OVERNIGHT AUTHORITY

How to win respect, command
attention and earn more money by
writing a book in 90 days

KATH WALTERS

TESTIMONIALS

Genevieve Hawkins, *Mentally at Work*

I would not have written my book without Kath's help. Her structured, pragmatic approach pushed me to achieve my goal with discipline and delight. In this book, her structure, pragmatism and a laugh along the way comes through loud and clear. We all have rich experiences that can be valuable to help others but only if they are turned into words. This book will help you become the author you always dreamed you wanted to be.

Jamie Pride, *Unicorn Tears*

I had this idea for a book that I couldn't get out of my head. Kath was able to extract the knowledge out of my head and drive momentum over a 12-week process that ultimately resulted in 55,000 words published by Wiley Business Books.

Leah Mether, *Soft is the New Hard*

I am a journalist. I know I can write. But Kath helped me determine the best book for my ideal audience. Even before the book was published, it added to my credibility and increased enquiries for training.

Rhonda Tranks, *Meeting Madness*

I just can't thank Kath enough for her help with the book. The structure is fabulous. The service is fabulous. I highly recommend it.

William Cowan, *Building a Winning Career*

Many of us find a way to start our book, but few of us finish. Most of us think we can write, but few understand how difficult it is to be well-structured, clear, and engaging throughout the journey. If you are keen to write a great book and are keen to finish it in 90 days, beg Kath to help you. She is not only incredibly competent, but also wonderfully kind, supportive, positive, and fun.

Mary Freer, *Compassion Revolution*

I thought about writing a book, I even talked about writing a book. I could have spent years preparing to write a book. Kath Walters has developed a program that isn't about thinking, talking and preparing—it's about knuckling down and doing the hard work to get the book written. Her guidance, structured sessions and insight ensured I had a finished manuscript in 90 days. My book is already reaching people around the world.

Therese Tarlinton, *Swap*

The energy and rapport I had with Kath from the start was a positive sign. She asked hard, in-depth and discovery style questions that gave me the comfort that I had found a great teacher. The first session about who the reader was and how this book was going to help them was one of the most dynamic and engaging professional experiences I have ever had. I left with clarity and purpose with a fire inside to start writing immediately.

Kath's structure, critique, questioning and encouragement were instrumental in going from a New Year's resolution to a published author in Booktopia within one year. I would highly recommend working with Kath.

Dale Monk, *Just Lead!*

Working with Kath as part of her Brain to Book coaching program helped me to calm the storm of erratic thought into a book that I am proud of. Kath's approach to structure, while not my preferred way of working, helped to corral my thoughts. Her flexibility allowed me to deviate from the plan and her support resulted in a great book that will help my clients navigate the struggle of authentic and impactful leadership. I had been 'writing' this book for more than five years, and it only reflected everything I hated about leadership books. Kath helped me write the book that I wanted to write.

Patsy Tremayne, *Study Less and Still Blitz your Medical Exams*

This is the second time I have used Kath's expertise to write a book using her Brain to Book in 90 days program. This time my son, Kell Tremayne, joined me as a co-author. Like me, he was taken aback by the incisive comments Kath was able to provide at each session. Our ideas were organized in such a way that each chapter was improved by her advice and insights. Kath provides great structure and is always upbeat, inspirational, and fun to work with. We have no doubt that Kath is achieving her vision to become Australia's most respected book coach.

Tracey Ezard, *Glue*

Kath's methodology tapped perfectly into how I work to get the ideas flowing freely. Her questions got me thinking more deeply, and I would never have found the structure without her. She's so supportive and easy to work with.

Leonie Therese Green, *Stop Doubting, Start Leading*

I came to Kath after a couple of false starts because I didn't know how to get it done. The book kept going back into the too-hard basket. Kath gave me momentum and asked smart questions, and her process really helped me get it out of my head. She was brilliant at drawing out areas where the book needed more clarity. She held me accountable and she knows what's needed to make a successful business book.

Paul Higgins, *Build Live Give*

Kath's structure is fantastic. If I'd been left to my own devices, it wouldn't have been so tight. She also played a great devil's advocate, so the book is much higher quality than it would be if I hadn't had that. Also, having times in the diary and tasks to do drove me to finish the book. Without that, a three-month process would have taken me easily nine months.

To my daughter, Audrey.

For your brilliant questions at just the right moment.

ABOUT THE AUTHOR

When the brilliant singer and guitar player Joan Armatrading toured Australia some years ago, she paused throughout her performance to give a little slide show about her achievements—the doyens she had played with, the kings and queens she has played for, the records and tracks that had achieved gold and platinum status. My point is that if we women don't claim our place in history, we will be written out of it. Well, let me rephrase that. I am not claiming a place in the history books but I am no shrinking violet.

As a professional business writer, I've written something like 1.3 million words over the past 25 years. As a business journalist, I was read by 40,000 readers a week for 14 years. My byline is familiar to readers of the *Australian Financial Review*, *Smart Company*, *BRW*, *Business Spectator*, *Women's Agenda*, *ANZ Bluenotes* and *Company Director*. I know what business audiences want. I know what they expect. And I have been giving them what they want and expect for more than two decades.

Today, in my work as a book coach, I guide smart, accomplished businesspeople through a momentous transition. They come to me as experienced, thoughtful practitioners. They have an idea (often many) like a mental itch that must be scratched. Getting that idea out of their heads and into a book is their gift to the world. And their book takes these experts to the next level in their business—a sought-after authority.

I am a self-declared 'finishing freak'—I love a deadline. Nothing thrills me more than the moment when my clients hold their book in their hands. Your book is a gift of untold value. I hope my book helps you to realise your dreams and help change the world for the better.

ACKNOWLEDGEMENTS

Of all the terrifying moments in writing a book, this is the scariest page of all. So let me start with the one person in the world who will not, I presume, be hurt by any missteps: my mum, Pamela Estelle Walters (nee Cliff).

My mum died in 1977 of breast cancer, just short of her 51st birthday. I was 19. Mum was a gifted violinist. She graduated with a Bachelor of Arts in the late 1940s, at a time when male university students outnumbered women two to one. Sadly, I never heard her play. But I thank her for her creative gene, her willingness to go against the grain and for the sensitivity that I have come to realise is also a gift. Mum, I wish you could have been here for this moment. It's these moments I miss you the most.

Dad, your tremendous energy and commitment to life and this planet often left me awestruck. I absorbed just a little and used it to power this book. I hope you and Mum are enjoying a bit of a polka now you are reunited.

Those of you who know my daughter, Audrey, will simply nod with understanding when I say, Audrey, you are my inspiration. For the rest of you, don't worry. You will soon get to know her when she assumes her rightful throne as leader of the universe. (No pressure, darling).

To the women in my writers' group, the catalysts who fired me into action. Di Percy, Yamini Naidu, Carolyn Tate and Sandy McDonald, you are all extraordinary women, leaders and authors. I simply could not have written my book without your care and companionship. How blissfully unaware were we at that first meeting on February 4, 2020 of the terror and devastation of COVID19. Yet we held each other through it all, staying true to our course and commitments. Dear women. Thank you.

And to my clients. To all those authors who trusted me with their creative hopes and dreams, I cannot thank you enough. Your hard work, feedback, willingness and dedication is the fuel that has kept me going.

What mettle I have was forged in the fires of your determination to stay the course—for me, for you, for your readers. A special thanks goes to Genevieve Hawkins, author of *Mentally at Work*, and Mike Adams, author of *The Seven Stories Every Salesperson Must Tell*, for providing brilliant feedback on my first draft.

Since leaving journalism and becoming a book coach and entrepreneur, I've met many remarkable fellow travellers. You are men and women of extraordinary financial, intellectual and personal accomplishments. You are people of grit and generosity. I met many of you (but not all) at the Thought Leaders Business School, for which I thank Matt Church and Peter Cook (who also first planted the idea that I could write a book). Thanks. You have all supported me in many ways. I am deeply grateful.

Amanda Gome is a journalist, entrepreneur and founder of the successful online business magazine, Smart Company. As a journalist and publisher, Amanda turned young people on to entrepreneurship, and celebrated and documented the value of fast-growing companies to the Australian economy. Amanda, your achievements are extraordinary. And, while achieving so much, you took the time to mentor me into business journalism. How typical of your generosity.

To Lu Sexton, editor of my first edition, great thanks for this book. To Liz Seymour, thanks for the scrumptious design of my first edition.

To Michael Hanrahan, Anna Clemann and all the folks at Publish Central, thanks for the editing and design of my second edition.

And to all my friends, my family, my dear ones. Because life is about more than doing stuff, it is about being accepted and loved through all the ups and downs. You do that. I love you.

Stick to it.

Kath Walters

First published in 2020 by Kath Walters.
Second edition published in 2023 by Kath Walters.

© Kath Walters 2023

The moral rights of the author have been asserted.

A catalogue entry for this book is available from the National Library of Australia.

ISBN: 978-1-922764-70-6

Printed in Australia
Project management and text design by Publish Central
Cover design by Peter Reardon

The paper this book is printed on is environmentally friendly.

Contents

CHAPTER NINE
Get Published
169

When, why and how to approach a 'traditional' publisher with your business book manuscript. 10 fabulous reasons to self-publish your book. To choose, consider what you want to achieve. Choosing an editor. Proofreaders. How to choose a book designer. The new printing options. In a nutshell. Over to you.

APPENDIX
Publishing Success Case Studies
185

Leah Mather. Peter Webb. Genevieve Hawkins. Mike Adams. Mary Freer.

Books Mentioned in this Book
201

The Remarkable Power of Finishing

In ancient times, an enormous sabre-toothed tiger chased a terrified man to a cliff edge. With no other choice, the man climbed onto a tree that clung to the edge of the cliff. There he dangled from the trees exposed roots, staring with horror at the jagged rocks so far below him. 'God,' he called out. 'If you are there, help me. I'll do anything.'

To his amazement, God answered his call. 'I am here.'

'What should I do?' the desperate man called.

And God answered... 'Let go!'

The man, stunned, thought for a moment and then yelled, 'Is anyone else there?'

Writing a book can feel as scary as dangling over a chasm lined with jagged rocks with everyone telling you to 'let go'. It's so scary that most people who start writing a book never finish.

I am not God, but I am a self-declared finishing 'freak'. I love deadlines. (And I hate deadlines.) Over my years as a business journalist at Fairfax Media (now Channel Nine), I became addicted to finishing. I wrote and published between 80,000 and 100,000 words a year. At first, finishing a story was a huge challenge. As a freelancer, it took me a whole day to write a 700-word story and more time to do the interviews and research. I just couldn't say goodbye to a story until I thought it was perfect.

And you know what? It was never perfect. Every story needed some editing. Sometimes my editor asked me to get more information, or check a fact, or clarify my meaning. Sometimes I'd been so busy refining the words, I added up some numbers incorrectly. Huh! Slowly, I learned the art of finishing and the incredible power that it had to change my life. And this is what I want to share with you.

Let me be clear—I'm not here to persuade you to write a book. I am just here to help you if you feel you have an important message to share with the world and you want to be proud of the book you write.

This book is for coaches, speakers and other experts who want to write a book about their expertise. It's narrowed to that niche because this is about writing a book in 90 days. It's not enough time to do much research. If you want to write a book about a topic you are not an expert in yet, you need another 90 days to research it. But if you are an expert in something other than writing a book, this book is for you.

I'll help you let go of your fears and float away towards a glorious horizon instead of crashing onto the jagged rocks.

Writing is 99% momentum

Did you know that Australian journos get six weeks' holiday a year? Anyway, I noticed that before a holiday, under the pressure of getting all my work done by the time I left, I could write a 3000-word feature story in a morning. I felt like I was flying. Invincible. But when I got back from holidays, writing a paragraph felt like wading through mud. I'd go around in circles. I'd second-guess every word. Was I a better writer before I went on holiday? No. I realised writing is 99% momentum. If you want to finish your book, momentum makes the difference.

Here's what I found finishing helped me to do.

Win respect

Respect starts with self-belief. One power of finishing is self-belief. Because I am a self-taught journalist and did not do a communication degree or a formal cadetship, I felt like an imposter for years. I wasn't a 'real journalist'. Eventually, though, I couldn't argue with the evidence. I finished stories every week that were good enough to be published in a respected national business magazine. An educated and discerning business audience read those stories. This would not be possible if I was not a real journalist. Ergo, I was.

Readers followed my stories and found them valuable. University lecturers used them in teaching their courses. Some of the companies I interviewed bought extra copies of my stories because they enjoyed what I had written (though some did not).

Command attention

I have never climbed Mount Everest or swum the English Channel. I'm a doctor's daughter from Canberra (don't hold that against me). But I learned to command attention by using the principles of journalism to write with authority, though not from the start and not on my own. I made many mistakes and some still make me cringe today. But I worked with talented mentors, editors and peers and I stuck to it. You don't have to be a celebrity to command attention, but you do need to share your ideas with authority. This book is about the skills needed to do that. Few are to do with your skill with words. I've seen journalists with slipshod writing skills get front page stories and win awards because they had great ideas and nailed the interests of their audience.

This book is about all the other skills you need to command attention with your book.

Earn more money

One power of finishing that I loved was making more money. I started as a freelancer, which meant I was paid by the word, not the hour. Because of my perfectionism, my hourly rate was pitiful. When I learned to get the story finished, my hourly rate climbed and then skyrocketed. Eventually, I could write fast enough and hit my deadlines reliably enough to get a job on staff at Fairfax Media. More money!

The killer question

When I am having a crisis of confidence, there is one question I ask myself to kick my butt. 'How would I feel if someone beat me to it?'

If you don't write your book, how will you feel if someone else writes it first? I've seen this happen to an outstanding expert, and it has happened to me. As a cub journo, I'd think of ideas and then dismiss them. Within weeks, I'd find them written by someone else. Ideas go away, writes Elizabeth Gilbert in *Big Magic: Creative Living Beyond Fear*. It's not that they get stolen, she writes, it is that if we neglect an idea, it will find a home with an author who does not neglect it. (By the way, I'll be mentioning a lot of books in this book. I've put a list of them at the end so you can delve deeper if you wish.)

Write your book in 90 days

As you may have guessed by now, one of the toughest parts of my job as a book mentor is helping my clients to finish their books and publish them. I understand how hard it is. It's impossible not to feel vulnerable about the words we publish. What if your research is challenged? Worse, what if you make a mistake? We are taught from our earliest days at school that making a mistake is unacceptable, shameful and embarrassing. That kind of lesson sticks.

Am I advocating making mistakes and not caring about them? No, I am not. You can become a finishing expert without lowering your standards. This book is about exactly how to do that.

In April, I clicked open an email from the international keynote speaker, Vinh Giang, and watched open-mouthed as he told this story about his father's wisdom.

'I remember the lowest point in my life,' Giang said. 'I had failed in multiple businesses. I was hanging my head and my dad walks in. I was down. He says, 'Do you know why you failed? You failed because you don't have enough soldiers in your army.' And my dad always uses metaphors when he teaches me lessons and he goes, 'Son, every single time you read a book, you recruit that author and he's standing behind you in your army. He's standing there with you in spirit, and son, the reason you failed is because you've got 50 soldiers and this battle you're fighting, you need 500 soldiers. This is why you failed.'

Be a soldier in someone's army.

PART ONE

FOCUS

BUILD CLARITY AND CONFIDENCE

CHAPTER ONE

Start with Who

OVERCOME THE NUMBER ONE REASON
YOU CAN'T WRITE YOUR BOOK

So many folks would like to write a book but can't get started. Or they start and get stuck. When I ask would-be authors what stops them from writing their book, they say:

) I don't know where to start.
) I don't know how to structure my ideas.
) I have too many ideas.
) I don't enjoy writing.
) I love writing but go around and around in circles.
) I'm a perfectionist.

These are all legitimate reasons but, in my experience, there is another reason. The true reason authors can't get started is this: they don't know who they are writing for. They think they know. But when we work together, they discover they have not gone deep enough to define their reader.

That's understandable. There is a reason they don't want to choose. This choice is one of the hardest to make. It goes against the grain for intelligent people to narrow down their focus to a defined audience. In fact, resisting the content of this chapter shows just how smart you are.

In a TED Talk with over two million views, scientist Alex Wissner-Gross proposes a 'new equation for intelligence.' He says, 'Intelligence should be viewed as a physical process that tries to maximise future freedom of action and avoid constraints in its own future.' I'd summarise Wissner-Gross in this way (with apologies), 'Smart people don't make a choice until the last minute'.

You want, you hope, your book will have universal appeal. You see more possibilities that way. But can you also see the possibilities that open up if you narrow your audience? Suppose you committed to writing a book for the vegan veterinary surgeons in the Melbourne suburb of Brighton. You write an entire book for them. You nail the problems they have and give them some fresh ways of thinking about them. You give them hope.

But wait. Now imagine your reader as the young vets of Brighton, 25-year-olds, who have finished their studies within a year or two. They work in another vet's practice so they can build enough skills to start their own practice. Compare the issues these young vets have to say, a vegan vet in Brighton who's 55, and wants to retire in five years.

The more precisely you narrow your audience, the more you understand the world from their point of view.

No one who isn't a 55-year-old vegan vet in Brighton will read your book. But every 55-year-old vegan vet in Brighton will see themselves when they read your book.

And you might find that the vegan vets of Brighton have a lot in common with other vegans, or other vets. Then you will have a much broader audience. But the vegan vets of Brighton will love you. They will feel understood when they pick up your book. It's like you're talking exactly to them. You must have this level of insight into the audience you're writing for.

Here's an example of a narrow audience attracting a large following. The *Australian Financial Review* is a leading Australian daily business newspaper that targets the CEOs of the 200 biggest companies on the Australian Stock Exchange. (There are many who will disagree with me on this one, but bear with me.) Its editors and journalists work hard to interest that narrow target audience. But around 2.5 million people read the newspaper. Other readers may want to be the CEO of an ASX200 company, or want to sell to those CEOs. They might be accountants or consultants to ASX200 companies, or might want to sell their small company to an ASX200 company. So the *Australian Financial Review* doesn't suffer from its narrow focus; it benefits.

A powerful shift of focus

If you are like most authors, you have a distraction that is impeding you from identifying your reader. When people come to me to talk about writing their book, most have focused on writing. (Duh, Kath. That seems sensible). Would-be authors may focus on how bad they are at writing, or how good they are. Either way, as long as they stay focused on writing, they stay stuck.

This is exactly how I stuffed up when I tried to write a book for the first time. It was 2015 and I was part of a group called the Thought Leaders Business School. I'd joined this school knowing I had to write a book. I thought (being a bit of a smart alec) that this task would be a walk in the park. As a journalist, I wrote more than 80,000 words a year. But I soon discovered it wasn't quite that easy. The entire project was overwhelming and I didn't start for ages. I hadn't yet worked out the system I share with you in this book. Although I knew about starting with the reader from my years in journalism, I didn't think about it when writing my book. Go figure.

If you are like most authors, you have a distraction that is impeding you from identifying your reader.

As the deadline for my book loomed, I panicked. I accepted a challenge from others in my community to write 50,000 words in 50 days. This I could do. I got up at five AM and wrote 1000 words for 50 days. I ended up with 50,000 words. I did not 'start with who'. Instead, I poured out whatever came into my head.

The result? You know when you drop a raw egg? Nothing you can do will save it. The same goes for my 50,000 words. They lacked any structure. It was too late to uncover the reader I was writing for, what I wanted to say to them and how to structure my message. That book remains unpublished. (But my program, Brain to Book in 90 Days, was born because of that mistake. Massive silver lining.)

The moment you shift from a focus on your writing to a focus on your audience, you reach a tipping point. At that moment, you commit to starting your book. Until you define your reader, you will stay stuck. It sounds harsh, I know. But I will show you how to reach that tipping point (which is the first of two). And this single decision will kick-start your book. It will put a rocket under writing your book.

Why I should have known better

I have been a professional writer and journalist for 20-plus years. When I first joined *Business Review Weekly* (BRW) in 1997, its founder, Robert Gottliebsen, was still with the magazine. He is one of Australia's most celebrated business journalists. From Gottliebsen, I learned that every story must have a benefit for readers. I had to understand my reader, so I could understand how they would enjoy my stories. It took some years. Even some tears. (Not all editors are kind. Are any editors kind?). But I got there.

For years, I edited the accounting section (don't turn the page). I reported the vicious competition between the four largest accounting practices, chronicled the ambitious mid-tier firms that nipped at the heels of the big ones and wrote about small practices, whose accountants had ditched time-sheets and lived happier lives. All three groups read my stories, but all had different reasons. And my readers differed from the marketing professionals who read the marketing section, the tech geeks who followed the tech section. And a different segment of readers again enjoyed the magazine features about Australia's biggest companies and wealthiest people.

'Reader benefit'—as my mentor, the entrepreneur and journalist, Amanda Gome, liked to call it—became my North Star.

Why did I forget this ingrained principle when I came to write my book? I'll never know. I'm saying, it is easy to do, even for experienced writers. But when I shifted my focus to the audience, I finished my first book—*Sticky Content: The delicate art of content marketing*—in 90 days.

Since I began helping experts to write books a few years ago, I've noticed that deciding on a precise reader triggers a profound shift for each of them. It unlocks a door to their creativity. This decision builds their confidence in the value of their ideas and gets them started.

When you visualise your reader with precision, you connect with how much these readers need your book. Your readers are the people you help every day with your expertise. You know you have an important message that really helps them. Reconnecting with that sense of conviction fosters an energy and excitement that will carry you through the 90 days you need to get this job done.

I want that for you. Because if you don't get started, you can't get finished.

Increase your return on investment

In my introduction to this book, I discuss the value of advancing from expert to authority by writing a book. I am not here to persuade you to write a book, just to show you how.

In that business model, you do not get a vast income from book sales. You get a vast increase in sales of your programs, your training, coaching, or speaking engagements as a result of writing your book. You are writing a book to move you from expert to authority. You want clients to come to you. Not just any clients—your ideal clients.

That will happen faster if you write for a niche. To substantiate this, I draw on the book by the American author, Michael Port. His book, *Book Yourself Solid*, covers off this idea in the first chapter, beautifully titled 'The Red Velvet Rope Policy'. He writes, 'Imagine that a friend has invited you to accompany her to an invitation-only special event. You arrive and approach the door, surprised to find a red velvet rope stretched between two shiny brass poles. A nicely dressed man asks your name, checking his invitation list. Finding your name there, he flashes a wide grin and drops one end of the rope, allowing you to pass through and enter the party. You feel like a star.'

Port encapsulates this idea of a niche audience with his red velvet rope metaphor. When you narrow your audience, you deploy the red velvet rope policy that he describes. Everyone who works with you, who reads your book, will feel special. What happens when your clients read your brilliant book? They recommend you to their friends and colleagues. That is how your book works. Your first readers recommend your book in this niche audience. News of its value spreads like wildfire.

Defining your reader is the first of two tipping points that will take you from 'brain to book' in 90 days: the commitment to start. (The other tipping point is committing to finish.) What is a tipping point? The *Cambridge Dictionary* defines it as 'the time at which a change or an effect cannot be stopped.' I love that thought. Once you know who you are writing for, no one can stop you—not even yourself.

I have a timesaving template called The Ultimate Guide to Getting Your Book Started. Ah, I love this guide. I'm about to take you through all the questions on this template. As you answer the 18 questions, you will discover who you are writing for and you will be ready for Chapter Two: Choose Your Best Ideas. Let me show you how.

An aside for thought leaders

Those readers who know the Thought Leaders Business School method may object to the proposition: 'start with who'. All thought leadership starts with ideas. Then you discover who your knowledge can help by conducting a series of market experiments. I'm not contradicting that approach here. If you haven't developed your ideas—your thought leadership—do that before you attempt to write a book in 90 days. Don't take too long though. You can research a book in 90 days if you need to do that (and I can help you). This book is for experts clear on their thought leadership.

The Ultimate Guide to Getting Your Book Started

Simon Sinek, the author of *Start with Why* is a hero of mine. 'People don't buy what you do; they buy why you do it,' he writes in this important book. It was a career highlight for me when I interviewed Simon Sinek for 'The Growth Faculty' book club in 2013. But back to business.

Why then, am I entreating you to start with who? Because I am assuming you know your 'why'. You are an expert. For years, perhaps decades, you've helped your clients make extraordinary progress using your clever ideas (also known as intellectual property). If you don't know why you do what you do by now, take a diversion and read *The Purpose Project* by Carolyn Tate. She will guide you to your inner purpose.

My 'why' has not wavered since I first graduated from art school in 1981. (Please keep that date a secret, ok?) I help people tell stories that help others. I can only see that looking back, however. I started as a visual storyteller, working with community groups to make silk-screen posters that told the story of their work. When I became a business journalist, I wrote about the challenges business leaders overcame to achieve their growth and success. No one likes a success story unless also you tell them about the pain the hero experienced getting to their goal. Otherwise it's just bragging.

So it will surprise you to see that the first four questions in the Ultimate Guide to Getting Your Book Started are about what you want to achieve by writing a book and why. Am I crazy? I'm contradicting myself already. No, I'm not. I have an excellent reason for asking those four questions.

Q1) What do you want to achieve by writing this book?

You already know why you do what you do. But you might not be clear about why you want to capture that expertise in a book. Have a good long think about that. You must be clear about your motivations for writing. The reasons experts tell me they want to write a book include to:

-) Start a conversation or debate.
-) Share the messages they know really help people.
-) Command attention in a crowded marketplace.
-) Win respect and recognition for what they know.
-) Stay ahead of competition.
-) Attract the right clients.
-) Reduce marketing effort.
-) Get the book out of their head (before they go crazy).

You may share those reasons. You may have others of your own. Write them down.

Q2) Why do those achievements matter to you?

This is a wonderful question that I learned to ask in a sales training class taught by sales expert, Rachel Bourke, from SalesSPACE. This question reminds you of what you value. Remind yourself of what matters to you and how writing your book will help you live up to those values.

Q3 ⟩ List at least 10 reasons these achievements are possible.

What resources do you already have that will make reaching these goals doable? This is a question that my coach, Dr Tess Bartlett, used to ask me when I first started out as a book coach and was full of self-doubt. By answering this question (often) I soon convinced myself of my abilities.

Q4 ⟩ Imagine that it is a year from now. How would you feel if you have achieved your goals by writing and publishing your book?

Picture how you will feel 12 months from now with your book in your hands. How will it affect your life and your business? You are on stage, sharing your message as a speaker. Your ideal client walks through the door—again. You feel a sense of accomplishment. You are proud to share your book with the world.

When I cannot be with you, these questions will be your buddy and your guide. Because no matter how systematic you are about writing your book, it will be challenging. The work, the self-doubt and the creative uncertainty will unsettle you. You will wonder why you started.

When you feel lost, questions one to four will reassure you. Read them. Re-read them. Write them on a sticky note and put them on your laptop or monitor. They are a superpower there for you when you need them.

Now for some juicy stuff

The next four questions will take you deep into your reader's mind. Did you notice the placement of the apostrophe in that previous sentence? There is a clue in that apostrophe. By the time you get to the end of these next four questions, you will have just one reader in your mind—your North Star.

There is a principle in writing that you start broad and go deep. Not too broad, but you start by introducing the topic and then you explain more about the topic. You start by introducing the news and then provide more details about the event and the people involved. We apply that principle here. We start broad.

Q5) Describe who you are writing for as if you were telling a friend about them.

Write everything you know about who will read your book. Include their job title, their gender, age, career history, marriage or partnership status, and their character or qualities as a person, such as whether they feel driven or laidback.

I've suggested you write as if telling a friend so you make it vivid and interesting. What brings this audience to life in your mind?

Q6) Now picture just ONE of your past or prospective clients. Just one who you loved working with. What are their three biggest problems?

Now slow down. I want you, if you did not do so in Q5, to write a description of that one person you pictured. Often, my clients will answer Q5 with descriptions like: 'a male or female leader in their mid-50s', 'CEOs and human resources leaders in ASX 200 companies', 'people aged 35 to 45'. That is fine. We must start somewhere. But there are vast differences between people in these broad groups. For example, at 35, I had a new baby and had not started writing as a journalist. At 45, I had separated and had a job with Fairfax Media as an editor and journalist.

It's difficult to capture a precise reader across a range of ages like that. A 20-year-old speaks an unfamiliar language to someone who's 55, full of emojis and LOLs. They spend their evenings going out, not recuperating. They get up late. They worry about the weekend ahead, not whether they have enough money to retire.

Try this. Describe the demographics of your friendship groups—mid-40s or 50s with teenage children, lawyers or artists or plumbers. Now picture your closest friend from that demographic. Describe that person. How much more vivid and nuanced is your description of that one friend than your description of the group?

Now consider your friend's problems. Perhaps he has a limp. Perhaps she can't give up cigarettes. If you studied an average 44-year-old bloke with two kids, you'd guess his problem is that he is putting on weight and can't communicate with his teenagers. But if that 44-year-old father is your friend, you're intimate with his problems. He used to enjoy going out to jazz bands with his partner but since he's taken on this role and the kids are teenagers, they can't get to a band. It's been ages. He's starting to lose a sense of joy in his life. This is such a unique picture. More powerful. More precise.

How to choose between two or more ideal readers

There are two ways to choose your ideal reader from among all the clients you worked with in the past. The first is to choose the person who has paid you the most money. I'm not saying that to be mercenary, but I want you to get a big return on investment from the effort of writing this book—at least 10 times what it cost you.

What makes this client an ideal reader is that they appreciate your value. They are crystal clear about your worth. They took your advice and acted on it. They recommended you to their friends and colleagues. This is why they are a superb choice as a reader.

I'd add a caveat here. If you dislike the client who paid you the most money, do not choose them as your reader. Choose a reader you like. The reader you choose must be someone you would 'clone' if you could. Given the chance, you'd be thrilled if they walked into your office again. And again. And again.

The exercises you are about to do with this imagined reader are powerful. You will manifest the reader you describe. Ok. Yeah, sounds kooky. And it's true: I cannot prove this one. Except that it happens to my clients. It's happened to me. When you picture who you want to be your clients, they materialise. Spooky.

So now you are ready. Choose one person and write everything about them, including all the items in Q5. Give them a first name, real or not. Use their name in that description. John is 46 with three kids. He's a warm guy with an enormous smile, but he has a quick temper and so on.

What are your reader's three biggest problems?

You are ready now to answer the second part of Q6. Ask yourself, when this client walked through your door the first time, what were the three biggest problems they had? As I mentioned, my clients say they cannot get started for various reasons. They feel like their book is stuck in their head that they cannot get out. They might have several books stuck inside. Ouch.

Use their words. How did your client describe their problem? Conjure up the words they used. Did they say, 'I'm exhausted from trying to lead my team. They don't want to listen to me.'

Resist the temptation to apply your knowledge here. My clients don't say, 'I am approaching this book with the wrong focus. I care too much about writing and not enough about who I am writing for.' They say, 'When I write, I spend ages trying to perfect a single paragraph.'

Your clients don't come in and say, 'My problem is that I don't understand the five Cs of effective communication'. After reading Leah Mether's book, *Soft is the New Hard*, they will understand that is their problem. But when Leah first meets them, they say, 'My staff behave like toddlers, throwing tantrums when I ask them to do something.' Or, 'I can't seem to keep my temper when staff respond to me.'

What are the problems that your clients describe to you? Can you list them? Write at least three. Try to make them three distinct problems. 'I get angry when my staff complain about their everyday tasks.' 'We spend more time talking about the work than doing it.' 'I'm under pressure from my boss to improve productivity.'

Q7) What are three primary causes of these problems?

Let's go deeper. You realise the cause of these problems is they don't understand the five Cs (or you would if you read Leah's book) but take it back a step. Don't rush to the solution. What would John see as the reason he gets angry with his staff? Perhaps he thinks it's because they are unprofessional, or too young. Perhaps he believes he's not tough enough. The reason for the time wasting is that John feels overwhelmed and cannot get motivated. The reason that his boss is breathing down his neck is that John has struggled with this problem for years, or that the company is under a bigger contract than in the past. Be precise.

Bring to mind the person you identified. Use their name. What would John see as the reason his boss is breathing down his neck? See the person in your mind's eye as you write.

Q8) What are the primary impacts of these problems on your reader?

What does it mean for your reader to live with these problems and not to solve them? I find the answer to this question ranges from the frustrating to the tragic. For example, my client, Jamie Pride, had a book stuck in his head. He decided what he wanted to call it: *Unicorn Tears: Why start-ups fail and how to avoid it.* He wrote a book outline with all the chapters mapped out. But that was five years before we met and worked together. It was damn frustrating for Jamie to have a book stuck in his head and an amazing accomplishment when he got it out and down on the page and used it to establish his successful consulting firm for start-ups. I'm thrilled for him.

For some entrepreneurs, not having Jamie's book would be a tragedy. They may spend wasted years on their start-up had they not read his book. His words may save their marriage or stop them from losing their home.

For me, if Thomas Moore had not written, *Care of the Soul,* it would be a tragedy. This book soothed, comforted and enlightened me. If Chip and Dan Heath had not written *Made to Stick,* I could not have developed my concept of sticky content (also thanks to behavioural economics expert Bri Williams for help with that concept.) If Matt Church, Peter Cook and Scott Stein had not collaborated to write, *Sell Your Thoughts,* I would not work in my book coaching practice today. That would be me not working with Leah, Jamie and others. Tragic.

What are the effects for your reader? What are the frustrations? What are the darkest outcomes for your reader of not solving their problems?

Stress test your choice of reader

Now you bring a deeper understanding of your reader and have chosen a single real individual to be the person to write for, sit with it for a moment. Challenge yourself with the question: is this the person I want to write my book for? If I wrote this book with this person front and centre of my mind, will they benefit? Will they find it valuable? Could I make a real difference to them with my words?

Perhaps you wonder if another person might be a better candidate. Good. Try the exercise again. Give them a first name. Describe them. Add detail. Write out their problems, their causes and their impacts.

Compare these two readers. Who is drawing you and why? My clients often start doing this exercise for the second time only to find there is not as much difference between the two readers as they had thought. There might be one big difference—their age for example—but in all other respects the two readers are the same. They worry about the same problems, with the same causes and impacts. But one will seem more 'right' than the other.

If you do this a few times and still can't decide on your reader, talk it through with a friend or colleague. Choose someone good at listening, not someone who will tell you the answer. Then listen to yourself. Can you tell who you are leaning towards?

Still not sure? Put your document down and go for a walk, a bicycle ride or a weekend away. Revisit your answers. Your reader is calling you. Listen. Then choose. Action precedes clarity, as Matt Church explains in his excellent regular blog, Talking Point.

'You don't get clear by thinking and waiting for motivation, you get clear by acting,' Matt writes with typical conviction. He quotes another brilliant author, George Bernard Shaw, who wrote: 'Life isn't about finding yourself. Life is about creating yourself.'

If you want to get started on your book, you must choose. The worst that can happen is that you will end up with a book that isn't right. And I doubt that will happen.

You are at your desk, obsessing about an enormous problem—how to finish your project by next week's deadline, for example. If I asked you what your problem is, you'd say, it is this deadline. Then an email pops into your inbox: forget about all your deadlines, it promises, take a trip to this day spa or this part of Italy. You click. The author of this email understands you better than you understand yourself. She knows your problem today is not that deadline. It's a feeling of overwhelm. A fantasy of looking more glamorous or going on a holiday is hard to pass up. That email writer knows your actual problem: 'I'm not feeling it today. I'm looking for a distraction.'

When you understand your audience's problems, it will show through in every word of your book.

When you understand your audience's problems, it will show through in every word of your book. They may be a little uncomfortable about how well you appreciate their dreams and their problems. Your book will be personal, as if written for them alone.

In the next week, watch the emails that hit your inbox. How many belong in your inbox? How many realise who you are and what motivates you? Which ones are you inclined to read and which do you delegate or defer? The emails you open are from those who understand you as their audience, they can cut through the noise of your busy life. As a writer, you want to be the email that your reader cannot resist.

In a nutshell

Narrowing your audience takes guts. As I mentioned before, your intelligence rails against the whole idea of narrowing your choices. You want to sell a million books. You want to build a million-dollar business or practice. You want more clients than you can handle so you can pick the best of them. So, narrowing your choice to a single person who will stand in as the representative for all your readers takes guts. But your audience will love you for it.

Now you realise why you can't start your book. You must shift your focus from writing. You've learned about the risks of writing for everyone. You've grasped the value of narrowing your reader to a single person. You might not get it right the first time so you stress test the idea. Do the work to pick your reader. It will rekindle your excitement about your book and how writing it will help you live up to those values.

In the next chapter, I'll show you the first reward you will reap from your gutsy decision to start with your audience first. And that reward is crystal clarity about your ideas, what to leave in and, even more important, what to leave out.

CHAPTER TWO

Choose Your Best Ideas

TEACHING THE PRIME MINISTER TO SCRAMBLE EGGS

Here's your assignment: write a lesson for the prime minister about how to scramble eggs. Easy, you say. You include the ingredients and the method. The tone of your lesson would be... well, I would have said respectful, but that depends on your politics. Whatever your leanings, you choose a tone to address the PM. And, for such an intelligent reader, you add some information about why scrambled eggs are the ideal breakfast for busy politicians. Knowing that politicians like to impress, you include tips about how to plate the dish and add the finishing touches. Alongside your written instructions, you have glossy photos of each step and a full page showing the finished dish.

Now, suppose I asked you to write the same cooking lesson for a four-year-old. With little thought, you would change the tone and the content. You'd include details like 'get a big mixing bowl'. The PM would know to do that, but a four-year-old needs more detail. You'd have fewer words. Maybe you would choose cartoons or diagrams rather than photos.

The outcome is the same: scrambled eggs. But you include different ideas according to the audience you are writing for. You do this with ease. Your instinct kicks in. You just 'know'.

Because you started with who, you will choose your best ideas with ease. Four-year-old or PM, it doesn't matter. Without crystal clarity around your ideal reader, you risk picking the wrong ideas or getting the 'voice' wrong. When you talk to a four-year-old, you make your pitch higher and use simpler words. Imagine if you talked that way to the prime minister. She would feel puzzled, if not offended.

When you know who you're talking to, you know what to say. Here is another example. You have a car accident. With your clients, you share a brief communication that focuses on how your accident will affect your work with them. With your friends or partner, you talk about the details of the accident and the emotions you felt during and after it. But with your four-year-old child, niece or nephew, you tailor the story so you can reassure them you are ok and looked after, and will get better soon.

Choosing your best ideas for your book wins the respect of your readers. Most of us know when we are going outside the boundaries, sharing too much, too little or the wrong information. This undermines respect. I recall a receptionist at one office I worked in who overshared the details of her weekend. If in doubt, share less.

Almost every client who's come to me in the last few years has had many book ideas. They have too many ideas for one book. To choose the best ideas we do what I have set out.

Step 1   Get clear about the audience—start with who.

Step 2   Use that clarity to decide which of their ideas to include in their book, and what to leave out.

Leah Mether wrote her fantastic book *Soft is the New Hard* through my Brain to Book in 90 Days program. Leah's book is about how to communicate well, especially under pressure. Leah has many talents and offers training programs to different markets. In our first session together, Leah shared two different book topics with distinct audiences.

Like many thought leaders, Leah had plenty of ideas to choose from. We worked through her ideas together, looked at each of the potential audiences and narrowed them down using the methods I outline in this book. Leah considered the factors raised in chapter one: how could she quickly recoup her investment of time, energy and money? We stress tested the choice of audience and looked at the top two book ideas. By the time Leah decided which reader she wanted to write for, she felt confident it was the right choice. And she knew which ideas needed to go into that book.

In this chapter, I will show you how to choose your best ideas. We will answer questions 9 to 18 in the Ultimate Guide to Getting Your Book Started. In the next chapter, you'll go deeper into them, but first let's get you clearer about which ideas to choose.

We'll look at the ideas that excite and energise you, the context for your ideas, your thought leadership, the value of your ideas to your clients and how you help them. Then you will consider how to group your ideas together and shape your book.

Destroy myths. Share messages.

Authors share a common characteristic: a certain level of frustration drives you all to write your book. You see people suffer when they make the same mistakes that you have made. And they suffer needlessly. Why? Because they are acting on misinformation—or myths. They don't have the knowledge they need to make the right choices, just as you didn't have the right information until you developed your expertise.

Authors burn to name those myths, to destroy them. They feel driven to replace these irksome myths with their valuable messages that help people, change people, make their lives better. At the end of this chapter is my Ultimate Guide to Getting Your Book Started, as I mentioned in Chapter One. Let's look at the remaining questions.

Q9) What is your topic in one word?

As a journalist, I asked many leaders the simplest question: 'What does your company do?' It was astonishing how many took 10 minutes to explain. Now perhaps they were nervous. Fair enough. So let's get there in steps. First, what is your topic in one word? Mine is writing. It's no more complicated than that. Is yours leadership? Confidence? Sales? Communication? Retail? Productivity?

Asking yourself this question has two benefits:

1. clarity
2. humility.

When you state your topic, you know what you do. You can tell others. You also realise you are one of many. It's tempting to want to build your status by adding detail to the topic. For example, I might bolster my feelings of importance by adding, 'My book is about writing with authority'. But reducing my topic to a word keeps me humble. Some pretty awe-inspiring authors have tackled the topic of writing before me. Approaching your topic with clarity and humility will make you a better writer.

Q10 and Q11

The next two questions go together. Q10 asks you to write out at least seven myths that drive you crazy. Q11 asks you to write at least seven messages you have a burning desire to share.

'Finding your voice' is an example of a writing myth that bugs me. Finding your voice is a distraction and the wrong focus for any author.

Why? Because it shifts your focus to you, to writing and to perfection. As you may have guessed, my goal is for you to focus on your reader. Then you find your voice without effort. That is the myth I destroyed with the story about the PM's scrambled eggs.

I loved writing that story. Destroying that myth was fun for me. I hate to think of even one more would-be author setting out to 'find their voice'. If I destroy that myth, I will save them effort, time and thousands of dollars. Destroying myths and sharing messages fires me up and it'll fire you up too. You will remember why your book is vital to your readers. These myths hinder them. Your messages help them. Your expertise changes people's lives.

My client Jamie Pride blew up 12 myths about entrepreneurship in his book, *Unicorn Tears*. These myths tortured him. Jamie saw leaders who believed these myths lose their health, their life savings and their relationships with partners and children. He saw them hurt people, and these myths also hurt him. He destroyed these myths and introduced his readers to a novel way of thinking about start-up success—the Hollywood Method. Ground-breaking.

You need that conviction and energy to carry you from brain to book. Writing a book is a big effort, let alone writing it in 90 days. Maybe you are already flagging. I had to move house between writing Chapter One and Chapter Two of this book. My energy flagged. Reconnecting with the myths I want to bust kept me going. Then we had a global pandemic. Even that didn't stop me.

Sometimes, by the time you get around to writing a book, you've lost connection with the myths that fire you up. It might be a while since you thought about them. If that's the case, think back to a time in your life when you felt that burning desire. Where were you? What were you thinking and feeling? Maybe you associate a certain smell or visual with that time. When you tune back in, it will all come flooding back to you.

Your messages are not the inverse of the myths. Don't be lazy.

Your messages are not the inverse of the myths. Don't be lazy. Now write the message you burn to share.

The low-down on the research you must do for your book

Q12 and Q13 ⟩ Have you read the classic book on your topic? Have you read the bestseller?

People often ask me about how much research they need to do for their book. Few experts need to do a lot. You will have much to draw on from your personal and professional experience, from that of your clients, perhaps from research projects you have done, from articles. The sources are endless.

But before you embark on your book, read or reread the classic book and the bestseller on your topic. If your topic is productivity, for example, the classic is *The Seven Habits of Highly Effective People* by Stephen Covey and the best seller is *The 4-Hour Workweek* by Tim Ferris. To get more up to date, check out *Smart Work* by Dermot Crowley, who adds his thought leadership to the topic.

Again, I must attribute my clarity on this topic to Matt Church, the founder of the Thought Leader Business School. Matt is an ideas man. When he sits down to read, he has two yellow legal pads at his side. When he reads an idea that interests him, he writes the idea and he adds notes such as 'Good idea and...' or 'Interesting idea, but...' That is how Matt describes thought leadership and I agree. He distinguishes his thinking by capturing the idea and looking at what he agrees or disagrees with.

I have something to add to Matt's idea too. When I started as a journo, I'd sometimes get stuck on a story. I couldn't get it down. Later, I realised that this was a sign I hadn't done enough research to 'have the story'. The story, in this case, is your overall view of your topic. For example, my client Leonie Green has a fascinating take on confidence and self-doubt in her book *Stop Doubting, Start Leading*. Her overall view of her topic is that we all have an 'I suck' story (or many I suck stories). She illustrates this by drawing on personal experience, that of her clients and the wisdom in her favourite movies, such as *Kung Fu Panda* and *Legally Blonde*. Leonie has done her research. You will know you have done enough research when you 'have the story', meaning when you are clear about the overall message of your book.

The Elements of Style by W Strunk and EB White is one of the absolute classics around how to write anything. *The Little Brown Handbook* by H Ramsey Fowler and Jane E Aaron is another. The best seller in my field would probably be *Everybody Writes* by Ann Handley or Joe Pulizzi's *Epic Content Marketing*. *This Book Means Business* by English writer and book coach Alison Jones has a title that drives me into an envy frenzy. I drew upon Jacqui Pretty's *Book Blueprint* to update and simplify my chapter template. We see further by 'standing on the shoulders of giants', to paraphrase the mathematician and physicist, Sir Isaac Newton.

In short, do a literature review. Start your book by reminding yourself what others have written on your subject. You'll clarify your own ideas and feel new confidence about what is distinctive about your own ideas.

You also risk plagiarism if you don't refresh your research of your peers, whether they are the authors of the bestseller or classic. You may find that you've picked up ideas you think are your own, but they come from somewhere else. That is uncool, but so easy to do. Because you are an expert your ideas are everything. Show the same respect for other people's ideas as you would have them show to you. (Could that be the 11th commandment?)

Grammar apps, such as ProWritingAid and Grammarly, offer a plagiarism function. It is only in their premium version. This function searches the internet for identical phrasing in your chapter. This makes it easier to identify and make attributions.

Research to avoid errors, too

Sometimes, when you seek out the origins of a quote, you find that your ideas are wrong. Is it true that one in five businesses fails within three years? Or have you just heard that so often you believe it? Does it cost six times as much to hire extra staff as their salary, or is that an often-quoted rumour?

The story of the kidney heist—guy-meets-girl in a bar, loses consciousness, wakes up in an ice-filled bath without a kidney—is an urban myth. Chip and Dan Heath start their book *Made to Stick* with this story. Not all stories that stick are true.

If you think your ideas are unique, you haven't done your research. All ideas develop from other ideas. So go to your bookshelf, or to your local bookshop, or to your library and gather the books that would fall into the category of classic and bestseller in your topic—be it productivity, leadership, writing or teamwork. Find the classic and the bestseller. Do an 'and/but' read or reread. Be like Matt Church with his two yellow legal pads.

If you think, 'I don't have time to read these books again. I've read them before,' turn off the TV for two nights. I'm a big fan of Netflix, SBS On Demand and all the rest. But turn them off for two nights and get your reading done.

Define what you add to the conversation on your topic

Your ideas grew, like flowers, from the fertile soil of those who've come before you. You know this from your research. For your book, you must define what you're adding to the conversation. That's the 'and/but' reading that I mentioned in the previous point. What can you add to the conversation and what distinguishes the differences you bring? For example, there might be rules around grooming dogs, but for

Grammar apps, such as ProWritingAid and Grammarly, offer a plagiarism function. It is only in their premium version. This function searches the internet for identical phrasing in your chapter. This makes it easier to identify and make attributions.

poodles you can't apply all of them because their coat is more like wool than fur. It can be that simple. It doesn't have to be earth-shattering. It just has to add to the conversation.

Q14 ⟩ In what ways (small or large) are your ideas different from other authors on this topic?

Think about the bestseller, *The Subtle Art of Not Giving a F*ck* by Mark Manson. This is a book about acceptance. Many authors have written books about acceptance. The Buddhist philosophy is all about acceptance. Manson's book stands on the shoulders of giants.

Start with Why by Simon Sinek is a bestselling book about purpose. The classic on that topic is *Man's Search for Meaning* by holocaust survivor, Viktor Frankl. *How to Win Friends and Influence People* by Dale Carnegie is a classic in the genre of success books. All are books that have built on past knowledge and, if they're in your area, you will need to refer to them.

It's what you add to your topic that will sell your book. If your ideas are the same as everyone else's, there's one thing that's as certain as death and taxes: you will compete on price. Think through what you have that's different to other people and how you solve a problem in a way that's unique to you. I don't want you to miss your uniqueness.

Here are some ways you can be different:

Original research

My client, the marvellous Annie Sheehan, wrote a terrific book on project management with a defined audience. It has brilliant tools to help her audience, who are the project sponsors (people who support a project within a company). Annie added something special to her book—some original research around the characteristics of the different project sponsors. She'd developed a delightful way of classifying them as various types of birds—the owl, the ostrich. Fun, and just like Annie to come up

If you think, 'I don't have time to read these books again. I've read them before,' turn off the TV for two nights. I'm a big fan of Netflix, SBS On Demand and all the rest. But turn them off for two nights and get your reading done.

with an idea like that. If you have original research, make sure that you include it.

The way you work

In my case, my distinguishing difference is around the idea that you can write a book you'll be proud of in 90 days. I propose that if you use my process you will need four or five hours a week at the most to get it done in 90 days. There are many books about writing books. That's my difference (or one of them).

Who you serve

Remember the vegan vets of Brighton from Chapter One? Your book will be different because you serve this audience. They share other concerns with vegans and with vets and businesses in Brighton, but your narrow audience will reveal enough differences.

A substantial addition to an established piece of intellectual property

Many of my clients have licenced intellectual property from experts in their field of expertise. After years of working with it, they add many models and methods to the original IP from their experience with clients. They then write about their original contributions in their books and make attributions to the original thinkers as they go. After all, every idea builds on previous ideas.

A method or model you have developed

Christina Guidotti, author of *The True Believers*, builds her book and intellectual property around several models. Her 'true believers superpowers' model creates the bedrock of her ideas. She devotes all of part two of her book to describing this model—what she means by the superpowers and how they influence your ability to succeed.

Christina inspired some of my thoughts about the tipping points in getting a book written. The first tipping point in a model I use with clients is: Commit to Start, which differs from the second tipping point: Commit to Finish. Christina's work on commitment helped me clarify these ideas.

Your FAQs

You might find your point of difference in the answers you give repeatedly to clients. The more you answer a question, the more streamlined your explanations become. Have you found a metaphor that you used to explain a sticking point? Do you jot down a diagram as you take clients through an explanation? Stay alert.

If you remain uncertain about your point of difference, ask your clients, colleagues or friends. Ask them what is distinctive about what you do. They will be happy to help.

A note for coaches

Many coaches feel they have nothing different to contribute. 'All I do is ask questions,' some coaches have said to me. They work with the subject material that their clients bring to them. Coaches are harsh on themselves. In my experience, most expert coaches have intellectual property around who they serve and how they do it. Often, they have developed tools and models that they used to help their clients too. They may not have fleshed them out with the depth of, say, Christina's model. However, writing their book is a chance to do that.

Claudia Lantos, my client, executive coach and author of *The Adversity Advantage*, developed The Scenario Thinking Framework™ to help her clients through adversity. Sheila Wherry, author of *The Pinnacle of Presence* developed clarity about her difference as she wrote her book. It lay in the sequence of building presence that she uses.

Understand the key value you offer to your readers

Q15) What is your key value proposition?

Robyn Haydon was an early adopter of self-publishing. On her shoulders, I stand. She wrote and published her first book while she was at home with her first child. *The Shredder Test: A step-by-step guide to writing WINNING proposals* opened the door to an additional stream of revenue for Robyn. She had been a contractor and consultant. Now, she trains others in her techniques. Her book got the whole industry talking. Clever.

To help you define the key value you offer your clients, I draw on Robyn's most recent book: *Value: How to talk about what you do so people want to buy it.* Brilliant title, don't you think? Who doesn't want that outcome? I sure do.

Robyn identifies six value drivers:

1. safer
2. cheaper
3. simpler
4. faster
5. better
6. smarter.

She groups these under the following categories:

) visceral value drivers: (safer and cheaper)
) logical value drivers: (simpler and faster)
) aspirational value drivers: (better and smarter).

Source: *Value: How to talk about what you do so people want to buy it,* Robyn Haydon (2016)

Try to classify the value of your ideas under each of the six value drivers. Do you cover all the value drivers? Where is the value clearest? If you feel unclear about your value, this exercise will help you define it.

The currencies of value

You can sort the value of your offer into four categories or currencies:

) money
) time
) happiness
) status.

Every expert offers all of those things, but your readers will value one over all the others. For example, my clients value their time, so they want to get their book done in 90 days. But the outcome of my program is authority. When you are the authority, your clients come to you. You can pick who you want to work with. Can you guess the currency my clients value more than others?

Everyone reads with a finely tuned WIIFM radar (what's in it for me). Your reader doesn't want to read your book. No, they want to put your book down as soon as possible. Make sure they can't. Make every sentence irresistible. Deliver on the promise of your book title. Robin Haydon's book is for those of us struggling to define our value. The promise is in the title and she delivers with her succinct and original take on value drivers.

Sometimes readers don't want to admit WIIFM. When your currency is status, address it sensitively. For example, I understand my clients want others to see them as an authority so they can attract work more easily. However, I know that you also want to help people. I'm not just flattering you when I say that. (Well, a little.) I'm positioning your need for status as part of your higher purpose. That is a consistent theme of every author I work with.

Define your value and explain it succinctly. My value is to advance you from expert to authority in 90 days. When your book hits the market, you become an overnight authority. It took you decades to gain your expertise, but the moment you publish, you step into a different league.

Try to classify the value of your ideas
under each of the six value drivers.
Do you cover all the value drivers?
Where is the value clearest?
If you feel unclear about your value,
this exercise will help you define it.

Keep it simple. Don't write a thesis. If you're struggling to narrow down your value proposition, talk to a friend or mentor. And the value you offer changes, which is another reason for writing your book quickly. When your value proposition changes, write your next book.

Do you know what your client's nirvana is?

Define nirvana for your clients. Nirvana is a Sanskrit word. In Buddhism, this word describes the ideal, the highest state. I am taking liberties with this word and I don't mean to trivialise it. I want a word that describes the place of beauty, meaning and satisfaction for your client. Nirvana is vivid with each of those possibilities. I hope your nirvana is writing a book you're proud to share with the world in 90 days. Is 'overnight authority' is an inspiring description of the nirvana you are looking for? (Gees, I hope so.)

Q16) What outcome can you help your readers achieve?

When you first answer this, write your description in long form. The succinct version will emerge from that. My favourite book about writing is, *Write like Hemingway* by Dr R Andrew Wilson. The author has summarised his reader's view of nirvana in his book title.

Try to picture what your reader sees in their nirvana. What are the tastes, smells or other tactile sensations of their nirvana? They arrive at work in a great mood, knowing people like them as a leader and ready to have a lot of fun. Cook superb meals in under 30 minutes every day. Communicate effectively under pressure. Tell terrific stories that influence others. Feel driven by a sense of genuine purpose. Avoid start-up failure. Write like Hemingway. Your client's nirvana will probably be the title of your book.

No one gets to nirvana without knowing where they are going. And no one changes without a reason. You need to define what your readers want to change and where they want to be. Nirvana is their aspiration. Don't over-promise or make it sound ridiculous. For example, Dale Carnegie did not call his book 'How to make everyone in the world like you'. Instead, he promises some friends and some influence with his brilliant title *How to Win Friends and Influence People*. Make sure the nirvana is aspirational, but achievable.

What are the milestones to reach their nirvana?

For Buddhists to reach nirvana, they must practise meditation. Milestones in their practice include sitting regularly, learning to sit for longer, observing the breath, developing compassion, giving up their goal of reaching nirvana. Let me steer myself to safer ground.

Even though you are setting a lofty goal, you know that you have helped people to realise that nirvana. You know your ideas work. Even the manual for your car has a nirvana, a perfectly running car. Every book has a nirvana. Sit down and write it. What's the practical outcome of taking your advice at its highest level? Getting precise can be difficult. So when you next talk to a client (your ideal client), ask them what nirvana you helped them achieve.

Q17) What are the steps they must take or milestones they must reach to achieve this outcome and solve the problems you identified at the start?

Let's look at the structure of this book as an example. There are 18 questions in my Ultimate Guide to Getting Your Book Started. Each is a milestone on the journey from not starting to getting started. This is a micro-level—how you get started.

Keep it simple. Don't write a thesis. If you're struggling to narrow down your value proposition, talk to a friend or mentor. And the value you offer changes, which is another reason for writing your book quickly. When your value proposition changes, write your next book.

The macro-level is to get you from brain to book. In my Brain-to-Book program, there are nine steps:

1. Start with who.
2. Choose your best ideas.
3. Create your book outline.
4. Flesh out your chapters.
5. Avoid three common writing mistakes.
6. Accelerate your first draft.
7. Review your chapters.
8. Overcome self-doubt.
9. Publish: edit, design and print.

Q18) Can you group any of your steps or milestones under broad headings?

Have you noticed that the milestones above are the nine chapters of this book? I can group those milestones under three broad headings: focus, create, publish.

Focus:

1. Start with who.
2. Choose your best ideas.
3. Create your book outline.

Create:

4. Flesh out your chapters.
5. Avoid three common writing mistakes.
6. Accelerate your first draft.

Publish:

7. Review your chapters.
8. Overcome self-doubt.
9. Publish: edit, design and print.

Even though you are setting a lofty goal, you know that you have helped people to realise that nirvana. You know your ideas work. Even the manual for your car has a nirvana, a perfectly running car. Every book has a nirvana. Sit down and write it. What's the practical outcome of taking your advice at its highest level? Getting precise can be difficult. So when you next talk to a client (your ideal client), ask them what nirvana you helped them achieve.

Don't worry. You won't oversimplify your ideas for your readers. You make your milestones memorable if you chunk them down. Can you remember all Steven Covey's seven habits? Few of us can. But you can remember that there are seven.

Remember your readers are not on your level or that of your peers. You're the expert and your job is to raise people from their level to yours. The broad headings or chunks don't have to be brilliant. Chip and Dan Heath, authors of *Made to Stick*, define sticky ideas as memorable and understandable. I agree. Make your milestones 'sticky'.

In a nutshell

With this chapter and Chapter One, you have answered all the questions in my Ultimate Guide to Getting Your Book Started.

You've seen the power of writing for a single person in choosing your best ideas. You have rebooted your energy by defining the myths and messages that bug you. You've put your ideas into context, defined what's different about them, what your value is and the path of realising that value expressed memorably.

The work in these two chapters is hard because you have to make so many choices. The creative part is coming up. In Chapter Three, you will learn how to make your ideas shine like diamonds by putting them into a structure.

The Ultimate Guide to Getting your Book Started

Q1) What do you want to achieve by writing this book?

Q2) Why do those achievements matter to you?

Q3) List at least 10 reasons these achievements are possible.

Q4) Imagine that it is a year from now. How would you feel if you have achieved your goals by writing and publishing your book?

Q5) Describe who you are writing for as if you were telling a friend about them.

Q6) Now picture in your mind just ONE of your past or prospective clients. **Just one who you loved working with. What are their three biggest problems?**

Q7) What are three primary causes of these problems?

Q8) What are the primary impacts of these problems on your reader?

Q9) What is your topic in one word?

Q10 ⟩ Write at least seven myths that drive you crazy.

Q11 ⟩ Write at least seven messages you have a burning desire to share.

Q12 ⟩ Have you read the classic book on your topic?

Q13 ⟩ Have you read the bestseller?

Q14 ⟩ In what ways (small or large) are your ideas different from other authors on this topic?

Q15 ⟩ What is your key value proposition?

Q16 ⟩ What outcome (nirvana) can you help your readers achieve?

Q17 ⟩ What are the steps they must take or milestones they must reach to achieve this outcome and solve the problems you identified at the start?

Q18 ⟩ Can you group any of your steps or milestones under broad headings?

CHAPTER THREE

Nail Your
Book Outline

TO CREATE A BRILLIANT BOOK
OUTLINE, USE THE WHY, WHAT
AND HOW STRUCTURE.

Before Picasso invented cubism, he learned to paint the old masters. He packed up his easel and his paintbox and went to the local museum. Sitting down in front of the paintings created over the centuries, he practised drawing, painting and perspective. Composers such as Beethoven learned to play other people's music before composing any. In the book structure I'm about to share with you, you will follow the masters.

There are many ways to structure a book. You can do an interview structure, a chronological structure, an acronym can form a structure (a bit naff, but that's ok).

So, why choose a structure when you start? Because the two most common traps for writers that stop you writing and publishing your book, are changing your ideas and changing your structure. I have seen authors revise their ideas and structure for years. What happens?, Nothing. The book stays unwritten. If your purpose in writing a book is to amuse yourself, that doesn't matter. But if you're writing the book to help other people, you cannot help them until your book is in their hands. That's why I focus on the reader in the first chapter. When your goal is to help people, you must write your book. Let's use a simple structure that is tried and true.

You may feel setting a strict structure inhibits their creativity. I disagree. The masters in any field are creative within a structure. Consider tennis. Now there is a structured way of spending time. But if you have ever watched tennis greats like Serena Williams or Rafael Nadal play, you will see creativity on fire in how they interpret the game. Creative within a tried-and-true structure.

Here's your structure: why, what and how

To create a brilliant book outline, use the why, what and how structure. Divide your ideas up into nine chapters. Three chapters about why, three chapters about what and three chapters about how. Stephen Covey's bestseller, *The Seven Habits of Highly Effective People* uses a list structure in his how section: the seven habits. But in Part One: Paradigms and Principles, Covey writes about the problems he wants to solve for his readers—the why section. Then he covers his research into personality and character ethics—the what section. Covey's why and what sections are much shorter than his how section. And you can do that too. The nine chapters can be different lengths.

If you're an experienced writer, you may not need this structure. But it won't harm your book if you use it. Dear reader, here is a challenge: commit to the why, what and how structure. Say, 'For this book, I will work within the why, what and how structure. I will not second-guess it.'

If you're a rebel like me and want to do your own thing, you might find that difficult. You are creative, a thought leader. You don't want people telling you what to do. For this book, calm your inner rebel and put it back in its box. Trust me.

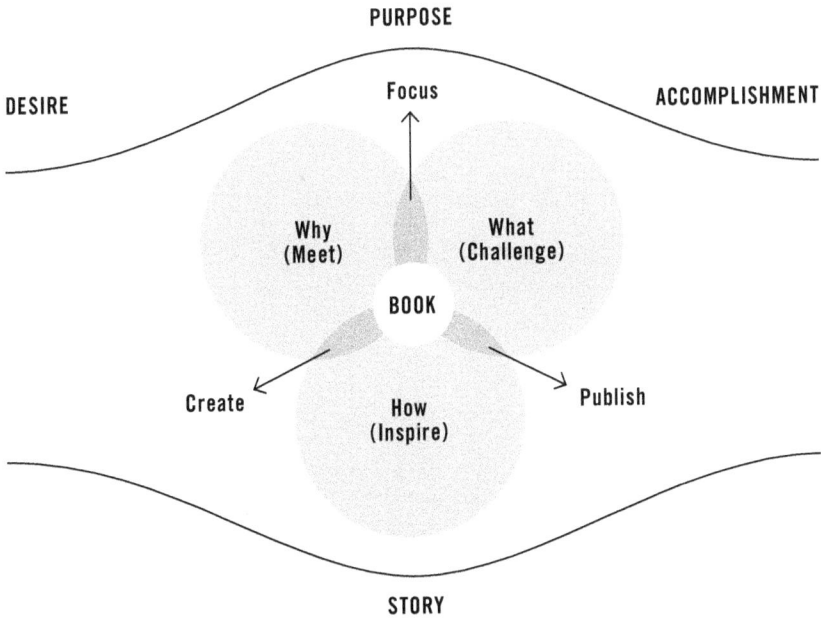

PURPOSE

DESIRE   Focus   ACCOMPLISHMENT

Why   What
(Meet)   (Challenge)

BOOK

Create   How   Publish
(Inspire)

STORY

Source: Kath Walters © 2023

Books are like babushka dolls—those wooden dolls that you split in half and find another doll inside, which splits in half to reveal the next doll. Books break down into chapters, which break down into subtopics, which break down to paragraphs, then sentences, then words. Within every chapter, every subtopic and sentence, there is a bit of why, what and how. Stay flexible. This structure is not meant to be a straightjacket that holds you rigidly in place. I mean it to be a cloak you wear lightly.

'Why' chapters

The 'why' chapters are where you meet your readers

The 'why' chapters remind me of when you meet a client for the first time. You sit down with them and draw them out about their problems. In a gracious and elegant way, you ask them, why am I here? How can I help you today?

In the 'why' chapters of your book, you meet your readers. You talk about the problems they have. You name their problems, which are the reasons they've picked up your book. You help them understand their problems by going into some detail about what these problems look and feel like. What causes them? What impact do they have?

Keep the 'why' chapters practical. The 'why' of every non-fiction book is change. People read your book to solve a problem they cannot solve themselves. With my book, the problem is writing a book. These first three chapters of my book are about the three biggest problems authors have—defining your reader, choosing your best ideas and organising those ideas into a structure. Those are the three big reasons most people become stuck.

With the 'why' chapters, allow your reader to deepen their appreciation of the problems they have. When you work with your clients, you show understanding and empathy. And you provide them with a diagnosis of what you have discovered about their problem. You listen first and then explain what you understand about that problem. Give your readers a detailed insight into what's been holding them back. In my case, I wrote about shifting your focus from writing to the audience, which will help you start your book.

Nobody changes without a reason and often that reason is a problem. In my experience, I only change when my problems create pain for me. Even then I am reluctant. If the change is positive—I fall in love—I enjoy change. But when I pick up a non-fiction book, a business book, I want a solution to the pain that I am in— not finding enough clients, not earning enough money, working around the clock, being single, being unhappily married, feeling lonely. There are plenty of problems that we humans can end up in.

When you want to write a book and you can't, that is a painful problem. Remember Jamie Pride, the author of *Unicorn Tears*? He had his book stuck in his head for years. He wrote a chapter outline, but he couldn't write the book. That is painful.

Strangely, even though as readers we pick up a book because of pain or a problem, we feel reluctant to change. Change involves effort on our part. Before I follow the advice of an author, I like to be sure they understand me. Do they know what my problem feels like? Do they understand my problem better than I do? If not, I can go back to watching movies and feeling sorry for myself.

Whatever problem you help people solve, give them an insight into the problem. Most of us are happy to read a book, but not to act on the information. We're even reluctant to read the book. If they've got any choice, people will put your book down. Keep them reading.

What is the primary message of your 'why' chapters?

At the end of this chapter, I share my Brilliant Book Outline timesaving template for you to fill out. Let's look at examples of 'why' chapters my clients have created. These will start your juices flowing.

Inspiring examples of 'why' chapters

The first three chapters of Leah Mether's book, *Soft is the New Hard* are:

Chapter 1. Do you have a people problem?
Leah's readers don't always know they have a communication problem. All they know is their people are not doing what they

should do. Leah explains how easy it is for intelligent, skilled people to find themselves in this situation.

Chapter 2. Communicating under pressure
Leah explains that most people are satisfactory communicators until they are under pressure. Then they default to old patterns. And, to compound that problem, most of us have no training in communication; we are relying on habits.

Chapter 3. Inside out
Leah reveals a fundamental reason that people struggle to change how they communicate: they believe it's a skill set. But Leah says it starts on the inside: with mindset.

Leah scopes the problem and sheds light on how leaders who are smart and skilled can struggle to communicate. These are practical insights that help her readers find the motivation to change.

In the 'why' chapters of *Stop Doubting, Start Leading,* Leonie Green examines doubt from three perspectives:

) the stories we tell ourselves and others
) the comparisons we make between ourselves and others
) the competence we bring to any situation.

Readers learn three of the essentials of confidence within the first 40 pages:

) communication
) comparison
) competence.

Leonie explains how leaders misunderstand them, and then how to get them right.

Logical Leadership by Jenny Bailey, has a terrific niche: engineers promoted to leadership roles. Her book has seven chapters (hey, not every book has to have nine chapters). Jenny captures the problem in the first two:

Chapter 1. The Makings of a Manager

Here, Jenny puts the case for learning management skills, explains why her approach is perfect for engineers (she is one) and then uses a wonderful tactic for a why chapter: she asks her readers to measure their own skills. If they didn't know why they should read her book before they do her test, they soon will.

Chapter 2. Stop Looking for Help in the Wrong Places

With compassion, Jenny reveals the reasons engineers don't have the skills they need: they are looking for help in the wrong places. She unpacks what is reasonable to expect human resources departments to do and what is not, why leadership programs are useless for engineers and why they should use their strength: logic.

How to write about your reader's problems

You have already identified your reader's problems in the Ultimate Guide to Getting Your Book Started. Before you go any further, go back to what you have written to remind yourself of the problems you outlined there, their causes and their effects. Within those problems you will find the 'why' chapters.

Flesh out their problems, the causes and effects. Don't rush to solve the problems. Expand your description of the problems before you shape their response.

Cross-check the messages you come up with by looking at the steps or milestones that take your clients to their nirvana. I guarantee the first few steps of your process will be giving your clients insights into why they have their problems.

Many authors struggle to write 'why' chapter messages. I did, too. Keep them practical. Don't be too literal with the why-what-how structure.

Cross-check the messages you come up with by looking at the steps or milestones that take your clients to their nirvana. I can guarantee the first few steps of your process will be giving your clients insights into why they have their problems.

Put down your ideas and then come back and see if they fit into the 'why' category.

Worry less about the chapter headings and more about the primary message of each chapter. I came up with the chapter title 'Start with Who' for chapter one after several drafts of the message. My message is this: 'Here's the number one reason that you can't write your book: you don't know who you are writing for.' I will give you tips about how to write ace chapter titles later in this chapter. Primary message first.

You will see in my Brilliant Book Outline that there is room for subtopics under each message. I will also come back to those later in this chapter. For now, start with the primary messages of each of your why chapters.

'What' chapters

Your 'what' chapters show your reader how to think differently

Your three 'what' chapters show how you think about your readers' problems. Share a fresh perspective with readers: your perspective. What is different about your way?

The next three chapters of this book are my 'what' chapters. I write about:

) what creates a strong chapter
) what the three most common writing mistakes are
) what a good first draft looks like.

Each of these chapters describes what I bring to the debate about writing books. These ideas set apart my approach from other authors tackling the topic 'how to write a book'. Remember two important aspects of your 'what' chapters.

1. **Contribute to the body of thought and ideas on your topic**
   Your 'what' chapters are not unique; they build on those who

have come before you. Other authors have tackled planning and writing books. I'm building on their work. You, too, must add to and contribute to an existing body of knowledge. That's why you write a book: to add to the body of knowledge.

2. **Challenge your readers**

You must distinguish your ideas from those of others by challenging your reader with new ideas. But keep them engaged. You don't want to be so challenging they put your book down.

A tip to help you challenge your readers without sending them running is to bring plenty of empathy to your 'what' chapters. The more you challenge your readers, the more you must show your understanding of them. Writing your book is one measure of your empathy. Who writes a book for people they don't care about? Not you. As a coach, speaker, trainer or facilitator, you have worked with dozens (perhaps hundreds) of people to help them solve their problems. When you work face to face, you show your empathy. In your writing, show the same empathy. It's harder in writing. You don't have the advantage of your facial expressions or your body language. You must remind your readers it's difficult to follow your advice. Remind them that, even though they are intelligent, they would have done it by now if it was easy.

Also, every chapter has a bit of why, what and how. Remember the babushka dolls. Don't end up too rigid.

Inspiring examples of 'what' chapters

When coach Claudia Lantos wrote her book, *The Adversity Advantage*, she included two distinctive pieces of intellectual property in two early chapters:

Chapter 2. Introducing the Scenario Thinking Framework™
Chapter 3. Shifting from high achiever to high performer

Every chapter has a bit of why, what and how. Remember the babushka dolls. Don't end up too rigid.

Drawing on her experience with clients, Claudia used these two distinctions to shift their perspective on adversity and move from managing to leading. With her high achiever/high performer distinction, she defines the two states and articulates which one to aim for, why, when and how.

In his book, *The Seven Stories Every Salesperson Must Tell*, author and sales expert, Mike Adams, has a four-part structure (no-one does what I say) based on a fishing analogy for sales: Lure, Hook, Fight, Land. Mike unfolds his why, what and how chapters a little differently. Each part has a why, what and how chapter. For example, in part one, Lure, Mike covers:

) Why use stories.
) What is a story exactly?
) Tell me how it is done.

In Mike's book, the four 'what' chapters are spread across the parts:

Chapter 2. What is a story exactly?

Chapter 5. What makes a connection?

Chapter 8. Be the only option (about what differentiates your company)

Chapter 11. Your buyer on remote control (about what stories stick in your buyer's mind)

Your structure need not be three why chapters followed by three what chapters followed by three how chapters. You can follow Mike and repeat the why, what, how sequence three (or, like Mike, four) times.

Your 'what' chapters build on a journalistic tradition

You may have heard journalists talk about an 'angle' on a story. There is a parallel here. I first learned to write nonfiction at Deakin University. My lecturer, Graeme Orr, walked his talk. He'd been a freelance journalist for decades. Graeme had written a story about buying an island. Every year,

Your structure need not be three why chapters followed by three what chapters followed by three how chapters. You can follow Mike and repeat the why, what, how sequence three (or, like Mike, four) times.

Don't go into lots of detail about what's different about your thoughts. You will become too theoretical. Keep it accessible for your reader. I might love my ideas to pieces, but you will only love them if they help you write your book.

he explained, he updated that story, came up with another angle, and sold the story again. He often tweaked it and sold it to multiple media outlets. At its heart, his island story draws on a popular yearning to escape the craziness of our world. What better way than to buy an island and retreat to its beauty and simplicity? Graeme wrote about people who bought islands and lived there. He wrote about those who had bought islands and wished they hadn't. He wrote about the price of islands going up and going down. He wrote about warm islands and cold islands and islands near the coast and far away. There are a million ways to write that story.

Every year, you read Christmas stories. How to buy a gift for the person who has everything. Unusual gifts. Cheap gifts that don't look cheap. Alternative ways to wrap gifts. Journalists find fresh angles on the old story of buying gifts. As I mentioned in Chapter Two, you'd assume *The Seven Habits of Highly Effective People* would put an end to books on productivity. Then Tim Ferris writes *The 4-Hour Workweek*. Dermot Crowley writes *Smart Work*. Done, surely. No, New Zealand businessman Andrew Barnes writes *The 4 Day Week*. Barnes discovered his 240 employees worked productively for 25% of their work week. When he gave them a day off each week, their productivity went up 6% and profitability rose 12.5%, according to a report in *The Sydney Morning Herald* by Anna Patty on January 12, 2020.

Don't go into lots of detail about what's different about your thoughts. You will become too theoretical. Keep it accessible for your reader. I might love my ideas to pieces, but you will only love them if they help you write your book.

The secret to your 'what' chapters

Go back to the Ultimate Guide to Getting Your Book Started. Look through your myths and messages to find your unique contribution. Refer to the classic and the bestseller. Have any of these messages and myths built on their thought leadership? If so, you will need to refer to them, explain what attracted you to this author and then explain how you arrived at the distinctions between your ideas and their ideas.

Go slowly. Don't rush your reader through these important points. Take your reader on the same path to understanding that you went on. Again, focus on your primary message for each chapter and give each a working title. I'll show you a hack for writing splendid chapter titles. But it's such fun, it is distracting. So, I'm not telling you yet.

'How' chapters

How to inspire readers with your 'how' chapters

Your three 'how' chapters show your readers how to act on the ideas in your 'what' chapters. These three chapters must solve the problems you outlined in your three 'why' chapters.

Writing out your chapters in a matrix can help. Create a table that is three across and four down. Label the top columns why, what and how. Number the boxes either across or down (depending on whether you want to be Mike or be me—nah, just kidding). It's simpler if I draw a diagram...

Your chapter structure Option A

Why	What	How
1	4	7
2	5	8
3	6	9

Your chapter structure Option B

Why	What	How
1	2	3
4	5	6
7	8	9

Writing out your chapters in a matrix can help. Create a table that is three across and four down. Label the top columns why, what and how. Number the boxes either across or down (depending on whether you want to be Mike or be me–nah, just kidding). It's simpler if I draw a diagram...

If your reader's problem is that they can't write their book, show them how to write a book. Every chapter in your book will include why, what and how information— the babushka dolls work in mysterious ways.

In my case, the how chapters are about letting go of your fears so that you can publish your book. You cannot win respect, command attention and earn more money until you publish your book. The most important part of the process is overcoming your self-doubt enough to publish your book.

Give your readers practical, prescriptive steps. Show them how to act on your knowledge to solve their problem.

Why your 'how' chapters matter

In your earlier chapters, you reminded your readers about the pain their problems cause them. Then you challenged their approach and told them they needed to change. Give them a way out. Inspire them to act.

Most coaches, trainers and other thought leaders feel very comfortable with the 'how' chapters of their book. To help their clients, they share the material in these chapters every day. This is their raison d'être. You know this stuff. Consider the people you help. You don't need me to provide evidence for this. You know this works. If you have any doubt about whether your approach to the problems that you solve works, I'd be astonished. You're an expert in what you do and you've seen the impact your approach has on the people you work with. I have seen the impact of my clients writing books in 90 days and putting them out there. I know this works.

Many authors worry about how much to give away in this section of their book. If you give away everything you know, will anybody buy your programs? Will other experts steal your ideas?

Here is what I know about that. There are three types of readers. There is the Walrus. The Walrus buys your book, reads it, loves it, and recommends it to all their friends. Then they turn over and lie back down in the sun. The Walrus likes reading and lying in the sun, not changing.

Then there is the Beaver. The Beaver also buys your book, reads it, loves it, and recommends it to all their friends. They do everything you say and achieve the results you promise. Beavers are DIY (do-it-yourself) creatures. They never pay for help.

The third type of reader is the (non-binary) Wizard. They buy your book, read it, love it, and cannot wait to work with you and buy your programs. They see the chemistry possible. They also recommend the book to all their friends, and their friends are the kind that will also want to buy your programs.

The big risk of publishing all your solutions in your book is that other coaches and trainers might steal your ideas. I have two thoughts here. One: once your ideas are published, they are instantly copyrighted to you (no fee payable). Proof if you are ever challenged or want to challenge another expert. Two, is that karma will get the thieves in the end. Their students will dob them in to you. And if they don't, the great protector of hard-working authors will smite them down. Whatever. You get more benefit from sharing it all. In the game of sales and marketing, the Wizard is what's called a qualified lead—a person who wants to buy what you're selling before you speak to them.

Do you spend time talking to people who have no idea what you do? The work you do is deep and complex. It's hard to explain in anything less than a book. You do it, I know. But when you publish your book, time dedicated to educating your clients can shift to time spent making them happier and more fulfilled.

Not every book has a big how-to component. Your book might be about why the world faces a climate emergency or about what is wrong with traffic design. But every nonfiction book has a how-to component. If your book is about what is wrong with traffic design, help readers spread

Remember to focus on the primary message of each chapter. When you have done that, you can use the headline hack I'm about to share with you.

the message by summarising the case for better traffic design. I'll go into this idea in more detail in the chapter planning section. For now, understand that you must decide how you will take your readers from problem to nirvana, and inspire them to act.

How to write your 'how' chapters

Go back to the Ultimate Guide to Getting Your Book Started and review the section about the steps or milestones that help your reader reach their nirvana. If there are more than three milestones, group some together. I explained this in detail in the last chapter.

Remember, stay flexible. Play with this a bit. Follow your heart and your gut, at least for the first couple of drafts. Relate the 'how' chapters to the 'why' chapters. You described three problems. Solve them with your 'how' chapters. If you are lucky and clever (and I know you are), when you drop them into a matrix, they will all line up together.

Remember to focus on the primary message of each chapter. When you have done that, you can use the headline hack I'm about to share with you.

How to write the world's best chapter titles

Back in 2014, I wrote a blog with the title 'How to use headline help tools without looking silly'. But I nearly called that blog: 'Responsible for the content marketing budget? 12 top-notch ways to spend your money.'

That second headline I had generated using a headline help tool. Then I googled my headline and found lots of other headlines like mine. Not exactly the same, but close enough for me to look like a not-very-original blogger.

A chapter title is like a headline. So is a subheading. Writing a good headline is hard—and important. Online, even if your headline is brilliant, only two in every 10 people will click on it, the stats tell us. Your book chapters and subheadings must be exciting enough to lure your reader on through your book, even though they have other more urgent stuff to do.

In this book, I have tested my chapter titles and subheadings using two (among many) free online tools:

1. Google Docs Headline Analyser
2. The Advanced Marketing Institute Headline Analyser.

Each tool gives your title or subheading (headlines) a score based on their own algorithms. The tools give quite different scores to the same headline, reminding us that a perfect headline is an illusion. But both tools help you increase the emotional content of your headline. That is a good idea because we are impulsive creatures, the brain scientists say. Our hearts rule our heads.

As I write, Chat GPT and many other AI writing assistants are causing a sensation. Here's what I got when I prompted one with the following: "Write 10 great titles for a book about writing a book in 90 days

1. '90 Days to a Published Book: A Step-by-Step Guide'
2. 'Write Your Book in 90 Days: The Ultimate Writing Challenge'
3. 'The 90-Day Book Writing Blueprint: Achieving Your Writing Goals'
4. '90 Days to Your Best-Selling Book: From Idea to Finish Line'
5. 'The 90-Day Writing Sprint: A Proven Method for Finishing Your Book'
6. 'The 90-Day Book Challenge: Unleash Your Writing Potential'
7. '90 Days to a Book Contract: A Writer's Guide to Success'
8. 'From Zero to Book in 90 Days: The Ultimate Writing Plan'
9. '90 Days to a Finished Manuscript: A No-Excuses Guide'
10. 'The 90-Day Writing Revolution: Transform Your Writing Process and Finish Your Book'.

Hmmm, I still like mine! But these are a great start.

At its simplest, a headline is a promise. If we read on, the words after the headline relate to the headline. At best, a headline is both a promise and also captures the problem: 'How to use a headline help tool [promise] without looking silly [problem]'. I got help with that one, too.

These online tools won't help you with a title for your book. They don't give high ratings to one- or two-word headlines. But they might help you with your subtitle. Here are five tips for writing chapter titles using headline help tools without looking silly:

1. Have something to say. It's a fail if you write a great headline, but the chapter doesn't deliver.
2. Don't take headline help tools too literally. Substitute words. Play around.
3. Learn the principles of good headlines from the generators.
4. Study headlines on the web that tempt you to click.
5. Google your headline before you use it. If it's overused, go back to the drawing board. But remember headline writing has always been a formula. No need to reinvent the wheel.

Complete your book outline with subtopics

To write an ace book outline, you need more than chapter titles and a primary message for each chapter. You need three to seven subtopics underneath each primary message. Think about these subtopics as if they were blog posts on aspects of the main topic. In fact, you might already have written these blog posts (I adapted a blog post for the section above.)

The subtopics must prove your primary message. You cannot have a primary message that says one thing and one or more subtopics that contradict your primary message. Remember the prime minister and the scrambled eggs in Chapter Two? Let's try that example.

If I asked you to write five blogs on 360° feedback, can you write a list? Now, does each one add insight to your overall view of 360° feedback?

Chapter title:

Scrumptious Scrambled Eggs in Under 10 Minutes

Primary message:

Scrambled eggs are the best breakfast for busy prime ministers

Subtopic 1:

Scrambled eggs are fast to cook and keep you going for hours.

Subtopic 2:

You make them using four simple ingredients you will have at home.

Subtopic 3:

The ingredients are eggs, bread, herbs and salt and pepper.

Subtopic 4:

Your scrambled eggs will be more delicious if you keep the heat low.

If I asked you to write five blogs on 360° feedback, can you write a list? Now, does each one add insight to your overall view of 360° feedback?

Now do this for each chapter message. Each 'blog' must add to and prove your point. But, I hear you cry, isn't it more creative and exciting to set sail and see where you end up? Not if you want to write a brilliant book in 90 days. If you wander, expect to take a lot longer than 90 days. You risk being less than brilliant. And you may never arrive. You need this structure or you will lose your way, repeat yourself, waffle, or jam it with information. It's like having a map without roads. It's no good having Sydney and Melbourne marked, without showing all the towns in between and the roads that connect them.

This is hard brain work. You do the hard work to help your reader. Each chapter takes your reader one step away from the pain and towards their nirvana.

Your reader is a busy person. They may not follow you down a meandering path. Most of us just want to start at A and go to B. If your book doesn't follow that route, your reader will say, 'See you later'. Let me hasten to add, however, that in my program, there is plenty of room for your creativity. That happens when you come to flesh out your chapters. And, in the last draft of your book, you can mess up this strict approach a bit. Move bits around. Play with them. But you must write your first draft to have words to be creative with. And creating a roadmap is the best way to write a first draft.

An important thing to keep in mind is repetition. When you plan a book and you have all the messages, it's easy to repeat yourself. That's okay—you *can* repeat yourself for important messages. If you repeat yourself, you always have to say why you're repeating yourself. You write, 'I've repeated this and I've done it for this reason.' It might be because it is such an important point, or because it's something people often forget. The only thing you cannot repeat in your book is stories. Once you've told a story, you cannot tell it again. It just looks like you've forgotten you already talked about it. Come up with fresh stories for every point.

In a nutshell

Now you have a structure for your book. It's not the only structure, but it's a tried and true one—three chapters about why, three chapters about what, and three chapters about how. When you create your book outline, each chapter needs a primary message and three to five subtopics that support the chapter's message. Think of those subtopics as blog posts.

Create a book outline that guides people from the problem to nirvana. Be flexible with the structure. Be light and playful. Your chapters may fall into the why, what, how structure after you've plotted them. Follow meaning rather than method.

Once you have written your book outline, share it with a trusted fellow writer or mentor. Ask for their feedback and change what you want.

Then commit to it. Don't keep refining your book outline and changing bits around. When it is good enough, start creating your chapters. Commit to your book outline. Then write that book.

Now you are ready to write your book. That is exciting. You have finished the FOCUS stage of writing your book. The next stage is CREATE. You will learn to flesh out each of your chapters using this Brilliant Book Outline you created. Nice one.

Your Chapter-by-Chapter Book Outline

This template becomes your book bible.

Your book title	
Your book subtitle	
Chapter 1 title	Primary message Three to five subtopics for this chapter
Chapter 2 title	Primary message Three to five subtopics for this chapter
Chapter 3 title	Primary message Three to five subtopics for this chapter
Chapter 4 title	Primary message Three to five subtopics for this chapter
Chapter 5 title	Primary message Three to five subtopics for this chapter
Chapter 6 title	Primary message Three to five subtopics for this chapter
Chapter 7 title	Primary message Three to five subtopics for this chapter
Chapter 8 title	Primary message Three to five subtopics for this chapter
Chapter 9 title	Primary message Three to five subtopics for this chapter

PART TWO

CREATE

COMMUNICATE THE QUALITY
OF YOUR IDEAS

CHAPTER FOUR

Flesh Out Your Ideas

ASK THESE SEVEN QUESTIONS
TO CREATE A BRILLIANT FIRST DRAFT
OF YOUR CHAPTER

When rough diamonds arrive at the cutting factories from the mines, they are pretty little pebbles. Until the jewellers sort and cut them, their true brilliance and potential is unclear. Before jewellers cut a diamond, they create a 'cutting plan' that details the size and angle of every facet based on the size, weight and colour of the diamond.

You are about to develop your chapters' cutting plan. Having narrowed your audience and focused your message, you have sorted your ideas into piles of rough diamonds. In this chapter, you will learn to ask seven questions that elicit the brilliance of each idea.

At the end of this chapter, I have shared my Brain-to-Book Chapter Plan to help you. Use the Chapter Plan, in combination with your Chapter-by-Chapter Book Outline, to plan out how to extract all the potential and beauty of each chapter until they shine like diamonds.

The best books go deep. That is why the first three chapters of this book narrow the scope of your book. If you try to go deep without narrowing your scope, you end up with too many rough diamonds. A friend and colleague of mine found this when she wrote a book over three years. The book reached 120,000 words. Then her progress was derailed by some massive life events. That much polishing would defeat the best of us. She might come back to this book. Meanwhile, she wrote another book, first narrowing her scope. She comfortably hit 50,000 words—an enormous achievement of focus and depth.

The seven questions in the Brain-to-Book Chapter Plan take you deep. Answering them for each subtopic shows your reader the journey of discovery you followed to arrive at your expertise. Consider the person you are writing for, your ideal client. When you first met them, they did not understand the ideas you will share with them in your book.

Remember, you are way ahead of your audience. Bring them, slowly and respectfully, up to your level. Your book outline is a roadmap to take your client from pain to nirvana. Your Chapter Plan ensures they cannot go down the wrong path.

Every feature story or article in a newspaper or magazine starts with a question or a proposition. Here's an example: 'If you want to live a splendid life and give back to your community, you must first build a successful business'. My client, Paul Higgins, explores this proposition in his book, *Build Live Give*. With great honesty, Paul reveals the 'frying pan moment' when he left his corporate job to start a business. The plan? To do what his corporate job had denied him—spend more time with his wife and children, do meaningful work and take greater care of his health. (Paul has a debilitating condition called polycystic kidney disease.) Instead, he found he worked around the clock, scrounging for whatever work he could get. Only when he discovered five 'growth drivers', could he clamber out of the fire and start building the life of his dreams. Paul shares these drivers to help his reader avoid his pain.

Pick up any copy of the *Harvard Business Review* (hbr.org) and pick any article. Here's one from April 2020: 'Use Your Customer Data to Actually

Help Your Customers' by Deloitte consultants, Joe Ucuzoglu and John Hagel III. Their proposition? 'What if your customers were eager to share their data?' It's in the third paragraph of their article.

Where are your diamonds?

The primary messages you created for each chapter and subtopic in your chapter outline are your propositions—your rough diamonds. You will create your Chapter Plan using the following seven questions for each subtopic:

1. What's your primary message?
2. Why should I care?
3. How can you prove you are right?
4. What might your reader say to dispute your idea?
5. Are there any exceptions?
6. How can your reader take action?
7. What barriers might impede your reader from acting on your advice?

But wait, I hear you say. If I follow the same seven questions for all the subtopics in my book, readers will find it boring and formulaic. Don't worry. At the second draft, you will introduce variety and excitement. This process is like setting out all the pieces of a jigsaw puzzle. It's infuriating to get to the end of a jigsaw and find you're missing six pieces. You have done all that work, but you can't complete the jigsaw. When you answer all seven questions for each subtopic, you end up with all the pieces you need for your book.

Deleting repetitive or excess content at the end of the process is much easier than discovering you have a piece missing in the second draft. Having to go back can be a stumbling block that sets your book deadline back. If the missing piece turns out to be a big one, you may even give up.

The Chapter Plan is not for you to write out your whole chapter. Not yet. You are creating the 'cutting plan'. Write your answers in bullet points. Then review each chapter for:

1. gaps in information or logic
2. jamming in too much
3. too few stories
4. missing sources
5. repeating yourself
6. diversions or distractions.

Your goal is to visualise the finished chapter from the plan, just as the jewellers visualise the finished diamond from the cutting plan.

The Chapter Plan is not for you to write out your whole chapter. Not yet. You are creating the 'cutting plan'. Write your answers in bullet points. Then review each chapter for:

1. gaps in information or logic
2. jamming in too much
3. too few stories
4. missing sources
5. repeating yourself
6. diversions or distractions.

Your goal is to visualise the finished chapter from the plan, just as the jewellers visualise the finished diamond from the cutting plan.

Chapter introductions

Before diving into the questions, let's look at the role of introductions in chapters. Using my approach, you will write the introduction to your entire book at the end of planning and writing your first draft.

Chapter introductions are different. They play the role of 'host', engaging and welcoming your reader into each new chapter. Introductions link each chapter and orientate the reader. They give readers breathing space between one set of ideas and the next. Stories make great introductions.

What if you arrive at an event or party and the host doesn't give you a sense of what is coming up and who else is at the event? Most of us feel uncomfortable if we walk into an unfamiliar space with no orientation. Are we in the right place? What is about to happen?

I'm guilty of skipping introductions. In some early workshops I ran, I launched into the content to grab everyone's attention. In feedback, participants asked for more orientation about what lay ahead. I realised I need to first hook their attention, but then come back and map out what they could expect.

The introduction is like the view from a helicopter. You can see the horizon and the way ahead. Don't get too detailed in your introduction. One trap is to expand on the subtopics. Just stick to introducing the primary message of your chapter.

For that reason, you will not find all seven questions in the introduction section of the Chapter Plan.

The seven questions

Q1) What is your primary message?

This question applies to both your chapter introduction and the subtopics. And the cool aspect of this question is that you already have the answer in your Brilliant Book Outline. All you need to do is add some definitions and context.

Don't frame your primary message as a question. It's much more powerful to make it a statement. Instead of saying, 'Can you write a brilliant business book in 90 days?' you say, 'You can write a brilliant business book in 90 days.'

Once you have your primary message, the definitions and context will flow from there. For example, what I mean by brilliant, what I mean by book, how a business book is different from another genre of nonfiction. Hopefully, there's no doubt about the meaning of 90 days. Well, except to explain they are consecutive.

You might assume some definitions are unnecessary. Must I define a book as 25,000 to 45,000 words? But people ask me that question all the time. How long is the book? You may capture some of your thought leadership in your definition. For example, I define a business book as one written to sell your ideas (and you), not to sell books.

From general to specific

When you introduce a topic, take your reader from the general to the specific.

Every chapter, every subtopic, every paragraph takes your reader from the general to the specific. News journalists do this. As I wrote the first edition of this book, amid the COVID19 pandemic, the then US president, Donald Trump, had made a gaffe in a press briefing by suggesting people could cure the virus by injecting disinfectant.

In reporting on the aftermath, the journalists, Harry Howard and Rachel Sharp, take the reader from the general to the specific in their *Daily Mail* story:

> Social media users have ruthlessly ridiculed President Donald Trump's suggestion that injections of disinfectant could treat coronavirus patients.
>
> Trump brought up treatments including 'injecting' cleaning agents in the body and use of ultraviolet lights at Thursday's White House press briefing.
>
> Twitter erupted after the president made the baffling claims, with one person posting a picture of Trump as if he was asking a boy mowing the White House Lawn, 'Have you injected your Dettol today?'

Don't go too general in your primary message. The story above does not start by saying Donald Trump is having a dreadful day. It gets straight down to the business at hand. No need to go back to the beginning of time to explain yourself or say something all too obvious, like 'the world is changing'. Stay focused on the topic you're talking about and add more detail to make it clearer.

Q2 ⟩ Why should I care?

Some ideas change your life. Yep, learning about the 'nub paragraph' changed me. I'd been a journalist for two years and couldn't understand why my editor wrote 'YUK!' and 'GUFF' on some of my stories (helpful, eh) while he let others sail through to the magazine unscathed.

I later discovered the answer: those stories were missing a nub paragraph. I will tell you about how and why to use the 'nub' in your writing. The nub answers the question in the reader's mind, 'Why should I care?' Without a 'nub para' in each chapter and subtopic, your readers will turn the next page or close your book. All your hard work, your brilliant ideas, your thorough research and your passion for your subject will be lost.

Sadly, readers are even tougher than editors. Of all the valuable tips imparted by the excellent trainer who taught me about writing features, the role of nub paragraph had the most immediate impact on the quality of my stories. I got a promotion to section editor shortly after completing her training. And I had much more fun as a writer.

Once you understand this idea, reading the features in your Saturday paper will never be the same. You'll find some articles don't have a nub para. But you will also notice many journalists who skilfully add a nub, and you can learn from them.

The nub para

The nub paragraph is not a secret. You can search the term and get lots of results. However, it is neither well understood nor widely practised.

Most experts define the nub paragraph as 'telling your reader exactly what your article will be about'. But there is more to it than that. The nub para must answer this question in your reader's mind: 'What's in it for me?' (WIIFM) or 'Why should I care?' If you are writing about a small business success story, why would your readers care? Perhaps your story holds practical lessons about how one business achieved success, or the business owner overcame their own personal shortcomings to triumph against the odds. You give readers help and hope.

Finding the nub of your story is not always easy. You make it easier if you are clear about the proposition you are arguing from the start. But the big reason that writers struggle with the nub is that they have not thought about their readers. The nub directly addresses your readers. You can't write a nub paragraph unless you think through who your book is written for. And this, dear reader, you have done.

The nub doesn't have to be at the beginning. An engaging introduction featuring an anecdote or amazing fact will hold your reader's attention for a para or two. Then you must deliver the nub or they will lose interest (even if they don't know why). Sometimes, a skilful writer can put the nub five paragraphs into the story. However, when you are starting, put the nub in the second or third para.

By the way, there's no nub in news stories. They hold our attention because they are current and the person, the event or the circumstances grab our interest. To keep us reading, the writer has only to satisfy it by answering the reader's questions—who, what, when, where, why and how—concisely and vividly.

The nub paragraph belongs alongside every proposition. You want to persuade your reader as soon as they encounter your primary message.

Remember to make your nub relevant to the subtopic.

Patsy Tremayne is a sports psychologist-turned-study-coach. She helps medical registrars ace their exams. These registrars are doctors learning a specialty. They pay up to $10,000 to sit their exams, so flunking is expensive and disheartening.

Patsy did my Brain-to-Book coaching program and published *Ace Your Medical Exams*, in 2019. Patsy is ace at the nub paragraph. Here's an example:

Energy regulation is your capacity to recognise your current energy levels and then control your energy when your body activates. The higher your body activation above an optimal level for a task, the more likely you are to feel a negative emotion such as anxiety. And the lower your ability to attend to the task.

Source: *Ace Your Medical Exams*, Patsy Tremayne

Now, Patsy does not say if you regulate your energy you will ace your exams. Her nub is specific to the topic. You will feel less anxious and focus better. Make your nub relevant to the primary message it supports. Don't default to why your whole book is important.

Q3) Can you prove you're right?

This question is all about evidence. Can you prove the point you're making? It's easy, as an expert, to feel convinced about your position. Somewhere along the line, you arrived at that position from doing research, from personal experience, from watching clients change, whatever it is. Include the evidence that persuaded you. Articles, books, research studies, your personal experiences and those of your friends, family and clients.

Stories are evidence

Business storyteller Yamini Naidu is a master of using stories as evidence. As Yamini shows in her book, Story Mastery: How leaders supercharge results with business storytelling, you can even use someone else's story to land a point.

> In The Cheeky Monkey: Writing Narrative Comedy, author Tim Ferguson shares this anecdote. 'A man sits on the train throwing biscuits out of the window. A woman asks, 'Why are you doing that?" "To keep the tigers away," he replies. The woman frowns and says, "There are no tigers in Australia." "See, it's working!" the man responds.
>
> Sometimes the tasks we do at work are unnecessary.
>
> Source: Story Mastery, Yamini Naidu

Stories are emotionally persuasive. It's a common mistake to leave stories out (more on this in Chapter Five). You must make sure the story has a point and is succinct, but tell it with whatever emotion was behind the story. Be they fuelled with desire, humour or terror, use stories, anecdotes and examples to illustrate your point.

Metaphors are valuable ways to press home a point. In this chapter, I used the metaphor of cutting diamonds to introduce my idea of polishing your content. If you struggle to think of metaphors, pick up a wonderful book called, *I never metaphor I didn't like* by Dr Mardy Grothe. You will have 314 pages of them.

And don't forget data and research. Bring in your original research if you have it, university studies, statistics—whatever you need to back up your point. Can you present such data in story form? It makes for a more engaging read.

Q4 ⟩ What might your reader say to dispute your ideas?

Cast your mind back to your first meetings with the client you chose as your reader. What doubts or objections to your ideas did they raise? If you get the answers to this question right, your reader will feel you are reading their mind. Think of this as a conversation with your reader. They may not have openly challenged your ideas, but expressed resistance, concerns, self-doubt, or channelled the fears of others, such as their leaders.

Let's imagine the former ABC 7.30 anchor Leigh Sales, one of Australia's foremost reporters, interviews a politician. She asks a question. The pollie answers. Sales then counters with a common journalistic opener: 'Critics might say...' before expressing a view that counters the pollie's position.

If you had just pitched your primary message to Leigh Sales, and she came back with, 'Critics might say...', how would that sentence end?

My client, Mike Adams, provides an elegant example in Chapter Three of his book, *The Seven Stories Every Salesperson Must Tell*. He is writing about

If you had just pitched your primary message to Leigh Sales, and she came back with, 'Critics might say...', how would that sentence end?

story planning and starts with a story about telling jokes with his teenage mates on bush walks in Tasmania.

'It's okay to recall a joke when it's triggered by another joke, but hoping a good story will come to mind at the right time during a multi-million sales is a big risk to take,' Mike writes.

He's answering an objection or doubt in his reader's mind: 'Do I have to think and plan my stories before I start? Can't I just wing it with my stories?' Mike does it with style. His point is even more persuasive because it seems to channel our inner thoughts at just the right moment.

Make these objections authentic. This is not meant to be an academic exercise. I designed this question to remind you to stay in your reader's shoes and see it from their point of view. When you come up with genuine objections, your primary message will be stronger for it.

Answering this question has a side benefit: it builds your confidence in your ideas. Publishing a book makes you feel vulnerable. Everyone's a critic. It's easy for others to take a pot shot at your book and that is an uncomfortable feeling. You stick your head above the parapet.

Of course, some criticisms aren't worth your attention. Some critics come from a place of envy or narrow-mindedness. They lack credibility. But some may have valid criticisms of your ideas. It's not possible to imagine every criticism, but it's worth trying. When you consider each objection your reader may have to the ideas you're proposing, you ready yourself, mentally and emotionally, for any criticisms to come. Anticipate and respond and you will diffuse criticism of your ideas. And, if you can predict what an envious, jealous or disgruntled person thinks about what you're saying, it's powerful to do so and invites a bigger audience.

When you step out into the limelight and put your head above the parapets, expect some rocks to come flying your way. It comes with the territory. When you have something to say, you will have someone who disagrees.

Q5) Are there any exceptions?

Imagine your book is about mindfulness. You explain the benefits of meditating to becoming more mindful. Meditation is useful for most of us. But what if your reader is clinically depressed or even suicidal? What if they don't follow your instructions and instead ruminate on their mistakes during their daily meditations? Have you considered these groups of people might be exceptions?

If your advice is to get exercise every day, should they check with their doctor first? If you want them to start a self-managed share market portfolio, should they have paid off their mortgage?

Have you ever taken a small child to a playground only to find they used the swing to hit another kid instead of to have fun? The right way to use a swing might seem obvious to you, but not everyone sees the world your way. Consider whether your point is relevant or helpful to everyone who picks up your book. Might some find it harmful or misuse it?

Or perhaps your reader needs most of your advice, but not all. In Chapter Three of this book, for example, I suggested that experienced authors might not use the why, what, how structure because they're experienced in developing structures for their books.

Be careful giving advice in your book. As an author, you have a responsibility to address controversial issues with some care.

If there are no exceptions to the message, leave this point out.

Q6) How can your reader take action?

This question sometimes confuses my authors so I must draw a distinction, which I hope will make it clear. When you write about how you want your reader to act, relate it to the subtopic.

In my chapter structure, every subtopic includes what, why and how (remember the babushka dolls). Notice a slight change in the order: you write your primary message (what you want to say), then why it is

If there are no exceptions to the message, leave this point out.

important, and then how. The how is a prescription to help your reader understand your point.

Knowledge is not enough. Most of us secretly wonder if we are the exception to the rule. Skilled authors guide their reader to test that belief.

Patsy Tremayne, author of *Ace your Medical Exams*, is also excellent at this. In Chapter Three, 'Recovery comes first', Patsy advises her readers to deal with their own stress and overwork before they set their study schedule. To help her readers understand this idea, she provides a reflection exercise.

'Set aside a little time,' she writes. 'Just sit in the sun, enjoy a break, and reflect on your situation. Often when people come to see me, it is the first time they have thought about what is going on in their life.'

Patsy does not assume her readers understand the stress they are under. She helps them to reflect on it. Her simple instructions guide them. Also in this chapter, Patsy provides detailed prescriptions. She includes a quiz, 'How self-assured are you?', so her readers can assess themselves. Later, she guides her readers to score their level of stress using scaled answers to 10 questions.

My client, Samuel Eddy, includes reflective exercises at the end of every subtopic. His book, *Fully Cooked*, is about recovering from burnout. He suggests his readers start a Burnout Diary. Each time he introduces an idea about burnout, he suggests a journal entry. His exercises vary from reflections to discussions with a friend or a mentor, or activities such as going for a jog. Each prescription is pertinent to the subtopic.

Do what Sam does—in your own way.

Q7 ⟩ What barriers might impede your reader acting on your advice?

As an expert, you have seen how powerful your ideas are—if people act on them. But human beings are hard-wired to be habitual. Behavioural economics expert Bri Williams, author of *The How of Habits,* provides a wonderful analogy. Habits are like an elephant walking through a grassy field, Bri says. The elephant carves a path through the grass. The next time she walks through that field, she follows the path she already made. Why? Because it's easier the second time and easier again the third time. Soon enough, the elephant walks down the path thinking about her dinner instead of where she's going. To forge a novel path, the elephant must refocus on the path, watch her step, keep her eye on her destination and stop thinking about dinner.

Our brains are like the elephant—efficient.

Trying something new requires effort. As an author, address the specific barriers readers might experience when they follow your instructions. It might be an internal barrier, such as finding time. Or an external barrier—the government confines them to their house during a COVID19 global pandemic and buying a journal is not one of the four official reasons to leave your home.

The magic way these seven questions supercharge your authority

These seven questions work like magic. Bullet-pointing your answers is like the cutting plan that will turn your rough diamond into a thing of beauty. Every facet of your ideas will shine, sharp with detail. Your reader will understand you and see the value of your ideas.

Your confidence in your own thought leadership grows as you answer these questions. Your book bursts with authority statements (your primary messages), proved by your examples, research anecdotes, metaphors, and stories.

At the end of writing your first draft, you will have all the pieces of the puzzle. Authors have found that, in using this process, they have to think through their ideas thoroughly. They notice ideas they've expected others to take for granted. These seven questions can be challenging. It is not because you don't have the answers—you do—but because you have to go back and reach deep into your experience to arrive at the answers.

This is a system, and it's an excellent one (if I may say so). It is a distillation of my experiences as a journalist, of my stories and the stories of others. Look at some feature articles or books you love. See if you can uncover the structure in the writing. Can you find the answers to each of the seven questions in the articles or the chapters you're reading? If one answer is missing, does it matter to you? Can you now see how journalists and authors flesh out their ideas?

Using someone else's system can be a challenge. It will feel awkward at first. But when you answer these seven questions, you have a way of making each chapter and subtopic substantial.

Use this same structure for every chapter. You can mess around with the structure in the second and final draft by loosening it up and moving the pieces around.

You might feel frustrated doing all this preparatory work. (I did.) You want to get on with the exciting part: writing your chapters. But this preparation will help you speed up your first draft, so you take less than a day (eight hours) to write 45,000 words. That's amazing.

In a nutshell

If this book was a jewellery box, this chapter is the diamond ring. It's the most valuable piece of intellectual property I own. I offer it to you freely to help you write a book that sparkles with your brilliance.

Use these questions to make your ideas deep and considered. Spell out for your reader how you arrived at your expertise. Show them the respect, care and empathy inherent in these questions. Guide them up to your level.

The system can feel stilted at first. You'll get better with the first few chapters, and you'll nail it by chapter four. When you have answered the questions for each chapter, you are ready to create all the chapters of your book in under eight hours.

But, just before you take that exciting step, I've got a chapter that will save you a lot of heartache. It's all about the three biggest writing mistakes and how to avoid them.

CHAPTER FIVE

The Three Biggest Writing Mistakes

AND HOW TO AVOID THEM

I am not obsessed with the skill of writing. Yes, I am a writer and I love writing. And to write a brilliant book, you must have some writing skills. But brilliant writing does not make a brilliant book. Well-thought-out and well-structured ideas make a brilliant book.

So far in this book, you have learned how to structure your book and then structure each chapter. And soon, you will learn how to speed up your first draft by recording each chapter and having it transcribed. You are carefully planning how to shape your rough diamonds so you minimise mistakes.

The three big writing mistakes that I refer to in this chapter are not about beautiful expression. Mastering these elements of style will not make you a poet. Of course, typos and grammatical errors undermine your authority, too, but I will show you how to address these issues later.

No, you will pay a worse price. These three blunders will confuse your readers. They will lose confidence in your expertise. They may not realise what is putting them off. Instead, they will have thoughts like,

Stories hook our hearts.
A book without stories is a rant.
It's a lecture.

'This person is lecturing me,' or 'I'm not convinced,' or 'I'm feeling lost. I don't know what the author is talking about.'

I don't want that for you. The three most common writing mistakes to avoid are:

1. too few stories
2. not linking ideas or chapters
3. overusing the passive voice.

When you overcome these mistakes, you will supercharge your authority. They are errors that you can correct or avoid. Addressing them will increase the quality of your book exponentially. You will also overcome feelings of self-doubt—the reason many people's manuscripts languish in their desk drawers. Authors weighed down with self-doubt do not publish. You will learn in this chapter how to address and overcome those doubts by mastering these writing techniques. You will emerge from the writing of your book with a more rigorous and deeper understanding of your authority.

Every book is a story book

And that includes your business book. We can convince with data, but we connect with stories. Stories hook our hearts. A book without stories is a rant. It's a lecture. It might even be a plea. A book underpinned by stories is like a powerful bird. On its mighty wings, readers soar above the problems they face and they see the patterns of information like fields of colour below. Then readers will swoop down to look more closely on a guided tour that you, the author, will take them on.

Malcolm Gladwell is a journalist and the bestselling author of many books, including perhaps his most famous, *The Tipping Point*. Gladwell is a master of persuading us by using stories. He's so good at it that sometimes I feel like he's almost a story bully. And I say that with the greatest respect.

He makes a point. He tells a story about that point. He tells another story about that point and then another story about that point. He keeps going until we, as readers, surrender. He shows us how this technique of telling stories provides the evidence that we as human beings need.

Everyone has a sceptical side. We might think, 'Oh, this story is about one person', or 'It's fluffy, and it's not evidence.' So you also need to address data and to provide evidence. But stories are not fluff within this context. Stories are evidence. They persuade us.

Going on a story hunt

In daily discourse, everyone tells stories without a second thought. They are our natural language when we relax with friends or family. But this is not always so easy when we sit down to write a blog or chapter in our book. Stories seem to evaporate when we try to find them. That is why I recommend to all my clients, when they begin to blog or write their book, they go on a story hunt every day and capture at least one story in an online story 'bank' or journal.

Not every story you tell must be your own story. If you are blogging, you need one or two stories per blog. If you are writing a book, you will need at least 30 stories for a nine-chapter book. The marvellous news is that when you look for stories, you will discover them everywhere. Remember, if the story is not yours, attribute the source (see more about how in Chapter Seven).

Here are seven places to look for stories to add to your bank.

1. **Your personal life**
   Make sure your story has a point. Only go as deep into your personal experience as you feel comfortable with the universe knowing.

2. **Your professional life**
   What lessons have you learned? The vital element of these stories is to make sure you are NOT the hero. (See more on page 105.)

3. **Your clients' experiences**

   Make sure you have their permission (they often say yes) or anonymise the story.

4. **Other people's blogs**

   Look for strong ones with magnificent stories.

5. **Podcasts**

   Every great podcast relies on stories. Buddhist teacher Tara Brach's meditation talks are a favourite source of stories for me. Another one I recommend is 'The Moth' where people tell personal stories.

6. **Newspapers and magazines**

   Look for stories that illustrate the points you are making. Stories from these sources add currency to your book.

7. **Friends and family**

   Use with their permission or anonymise. This is probably one of the more delicate sources of stories, so tread carefully when collecting stories from friends and family.

Bonus secret place: jokes

Consider funny stories. Too often—and I am guilty of this—the stories and examples I choose are too serious. Lighten up. Google jokes on your topic. Listen out for funny stories.

How to capture stories in your bank

Stories can seem vivid when you experience or remember them, but unless you capture the essentials of them, you might forget the point. So capture at a minimum:

1. **The story itself in one or two lines**

   For example, my older brother, at age five, broke his front tooth while attempting to put on his underpants with a single jump.

He missed one of the leg holes and fell onto a bedside table, chipping his tooth.

2. **The source**

   Did you read the story in the paper, did you hear it from a friend? Which friend? Which paper? The story of my brother's front tooth is family lore and retold many times.

3. **The point of the story**

   Every story in a nonfiction book must have a purpose or point. In my mind, my brother's story has many possibilities. For example, 'Learning can be painful,' or 'wonderful inspiration may include a practical downside,' or 'when attempting a fabulous goal, make sure there is nothing dangerous nearby.'

My friend and expert storyteller, Yamini Naidu, has a remarkable story bank, but Yamini doesn't worry about what point she might make with her stories when she captures them. She stores them in Evernote and applies tags so she can search through her bank. She worries about the point of the story later. But she always includes a point when she uses a story in a talk or one of her books.

Remember, stories hook your reader emotionally and so we must create a bank of them. Go forth and hunt down stories for your blog and book.

Don't make yourself the hero of your story

Unless you are my close friend or family, I am not interested in your personal successes and triumphs. To be brutally honest, if you brag in your book, I will start to dislike you. Matt Church, in his book, *Speakership: The art of oration, the science of influence*, expresses this idea thus: 'Don't be the hero of your story'.

Bragging in your book encourages other people to compare their life with yours and decide yours is better. Is that how you want your readers to feel? How many times are you allowed to brag about your successes, write about receiving awards, being given a standing ovation? Zero. Zilch. Nada. (That applies to social media, too.) Never make yourself the hero. Make your client the hero, your family, society, your clan.

How do you tell personal stories then? Be the fool. Tell the stories of your stuff-ups, moments of vulnerability and indecision. I make an exception in the introduction to your book and in the 'About the author' segments. You can claim your qualifications, expertise and experience here in a matter-of-fact way. Don't overdo it. Or underdo it. False modesty can be off-putting, too.

Your success is implicit. Have you read *Angela's Ashes*, the 1996 memoir by the Irish-American author Frank McCourt? While I found it hard reading about the privations and abuses McCourt suffered through his childhood, I knew he pulled through because he became a successful author. That made it bearable.

How to link all the ideas in your chapters to make a cohesive book

Reading a book should be like floating gently down a river towards an ocean of possibilities. To keep your reader receptive to your ideas, you want them to be 'in the zone', effortlessly connecting with what you say and gliding from one idea to the next. Yes, you want them to be excited and busting to get to the end of the journey. But you want the ride to go without a hitch.

How do we, as authors, achieve this smooth ride? Most people think the answer lies in having a quality boat, meaning we must improve our capacity as writers to lull our readers with persuasive prose. I disagree. Even a rickety old boat can afford a lovely ride if it is skilfully captained away from snags, whirlpools and rocks. Your focus needs to be on the river and steering your course. How? By making elegant links between all your ideas.

Jerky connections between ideas snag our reader's attention. Snags distract them from thinking about a problem they have, a mistake they have made, or an exciting course of action that you recommend. Instead, they think, 'Huh? What happened there?' If you are lucky, they push on and keep going down the river. More often, they disembark, flinging your book onto the couch with a sigh and thinking, 'I must empty the dishwasher! No excuse now!'

But here is the good news! You are already a master of the elegant link, the segue, the smooth transition between one idea and the next. You use them in conversation all the time. Here's some you might recognise:

'Enough about you, let's talk about me!'

'Talking of which ...'

'Any questions?'

'I am not a racist, but ...' (Yes, links can be used for evil as well as good).

We link ideas in conversation without much effort. We are also alert to breaches: you say hello to someone and they don't reply, or they launch into a topic without introduction—that is a breach. It can be offensive at worst and off-putting at best.

A mysterious problem with writing down ideas

Strangely, many authors struggle to conjure up this natural ability when they write their thoughts down. Instead, their ideas hop about like a cat on a hot tin roof. They become anxious about how to convey their ideas and link them all together.

Solving this struggle, then, is as simple as tuning into your 'conversational mind'. What do I mean by that? I mean that authors need to imagine they are talking with their readers. You might have noticed my conversational style in this book. How do I link my ideas? I ask questions, tell stories, and I use humour and repetition. In my blogs and books, I want to have an informal conversation with my reader. But you can write more formally, and still make it conversational enough to link your ideas. Just use the linking phrases and techniques, such as humour, repetition, questions or stories.

However, the links between your ideas need to be strong. A weak link is as bad as no link. If you cannot yet take to the page without a flutter of anxiety and you like to walk before you fly (an excellent idea), I have a suggestion: use a technique to help you actively link ideas. I call the method, 'Because of this, then that'.

Because of this, then that

You can test the strength of the links between your ideas in a chapter, or chapters in a book as a cohesive whole by asking yourself a simple question: 'Because of this, then what?' First, set your overall topics (mine is 'links'), then decide your subtopics. These are all the components that make up your topic. Now test the strength of the links between your ideas.

Here's how my ideas link in this segment of my book:

〉 Because your reader is 'in the flow', they absorb your ideas.
〉 Because your ideas are linked, your readers are in the flow.
〉 Because your ideas are not linked, they are jerky.
〉 Because they are jerky, the reader gets snagged and stops reading.
〉 Because you are talking, you know how to link ideas effortlessly.
〉 Because you are writing, you forget how to link ideas.
〉 Because you remember to have a conversation with your reader as you write, your links come effortlessly.
〉 Because you must practise remembering, start with an artifice.
〉 Because you use an artifice, you can link written ideas.
〉 Because you link your written ideas, your reader will get in the flow and absorb your ideas.

How long is a chain?

You can link one idea to another forever, by the way. However, you have a deadline, don't you, and have to get your book published and out to your readers. If you want your readers to be in the flow and ready to absorb your ideas, learn to link your thoughts as you write. Use the same links you use effortlessly in conversation—questions, humour, repetition and stories. Until you get terrific at that, use the 'Because of this, then that' technique to link your ideas.

Lessons from a chocolate-brown poodle about active voice

A few years ago, a chocolate-brown poodle ran in front of my push bike and I couldn't stop in time. I fell off and ended up in a hospital. The doctors diagnosed a broken wrist and lacerations (horrid gashes) to my knee and my forearm. Ouch. The chocolate-brown poodle escaped without a scratch.

I am not writing this to bring a tear to your eye. (Well, a little.) No, I wrote these first couple of paragraphs to give you a grammar lesson in the active voice. Since most of us have forgotten our school teacher's lessons on active and passive voice, I'd like to remind you!

) **Active voice** tells us up front who did the action: *The doctors diagnosed a broken wrist.*

) **Passive voice** leaves the who to the end: *A broken wrist was diagnosed by the doctors.* Or even leaves it out altogether: *A broken wrist was diagnosed.*

The actor's friend

I love the active voice. I like its lack of ambiguity. It's all about who does what to whom. When you write using the active voice, you emphasise the person (or poodle) responsible for the action.

Active voice carries the reader through your ideas. It's vivid. Clear. Often short. Active voice can seem blunt, but I'd prefer to say forthright. It carries more emotion. There is an immediacy, a sense of being on the spot, which is why reporters learn to write in the active voice.

The politician's friend

Politicians love the passive voice. Not, 'Yes, I stuffed up.' Instead, 'Yes, there was a mistake made.'

But the passive voice is not wrong. It's terrific when you want to:

1. **Emphasise the action and not the actors**

   'I was knocked off my bike.' Who cares how?

2. **Be polite**

   Because it's less direct, the passive voice can soften a point you are making. 'This could benefit from a rewrite,' instead of, 'You need to rewrite this'.

3. **Be ambiguous**

   It's helpful when you are building some suspense. 'The answer was not what I was hoping for.'

4. **Be less emotive**

   Such as with writing up a report of a car accident for an insurance claim. 'The car door was dented by the collision.'

5. **Distance the reader from the topic**

   Sometimes we want to take the heat out of our argument. 'These ideas are controversial in some circles.'

6. **Slow the pace**

   Long sentences and passive voice both slow the pace of writing.

So there you have six uses of the passive voice.

Active voice carries the reader through your ideas.

When passive is a pain

So when is passive the wrong choice? When it's working against the intention or tone of your writing. When you review your first draft, ask yourself some questions to decide if you have chosen the passive voice correctly.

> Did I choose the passive voice or did I use it without thinking?

> Do I want to create an emotional connection with the reader (active voice) or am I trying to calm their emotional responses (passive voice)?

> Am I addressing an audience that is sensitive to status? Do I need to be polite and tactful with them?

> Could my reader feel confused about who did what to whom? For example: 'A woman and a bike rider are crossing the road. She is hurt.'

> Am I covering up for lack of knowledge by using the passive voice? For example, 'Electricity was invented in the 19th century.' (You don't know who invented electricity.)

> Am I covering up for lack of courage by using the passive voice? For example: 'Actions have been taken that have affected sales in our company.' (You won't say who took the damaging actions.)

> Do I use the passive voice in more than about 10% of my written work? Above this level, your reader will struggle to understand you. If it's important to them, they will continue to read. Many more will give up. By the way, there are several apps that help you to spot and correct passive voice, which I discuss in Chapter Seven.

In a nutshell

There are three common mistakes you can make as a writer. You could leave out stories, you could not link your ideas and chapters, and you could write over 10% of your book using the passive voice. When you address these common weaknesses in writing, you will improve your book's influence and persuasiveness. It can feel like a lot of work to find and tell the stories, link your ideas together and carefully choose between active and passive voice. But your stories will engage the hearts and minds of your reader, links will smooth their ride, and judicious use of the passive voice will keep them reading.

Take these tips lightly, play with them and have some fun. Then you can proceed to one of the most powerful techniques that I have for you to get your book out into the world in 90 days—accelerating your first draft and saving you at least 75% of your writing time. I cover this in the next chapter.

CHAPTER SIX

Writing at a Gallop

WHEN YOU RECORD YOUR FIRST DRAFT,
YOU CUT YOUR WRITING TIME BY 75%

I wrote the first draft of this chapter sitting on a banana chair in the sunshine on my back deck. I didn't have my laptop, just my iPad, open to my preparation for the chapter. For about 45 minutes, I asked myself the questions on the Chapter Plan and talked through the answers, based on my dot points. All the while, I recorded everything I said on my iPhone, using a free app called Rev. 'Kath,' I said to myself. 'What is the primary message of this chapter?' 'Well Kath, this chapter is all about writing at a gallop. It is about how to record your first draft and save yourself 75% of the time it would take if you were to type it.' Not sure what the neighbours thought.

Blank pages can be intimidating, horrifying and scary for authors. And writing can be very slow. Even if you can type quickly, it's hard to think and write at the same time. Talking and recording solves that problem. I call this writing at a gallop. There is a bit of a knack to this method, but it means you can capture about 4,500 words in 30 to 45 minutes. I've been writing for decades and I cannot write 4,500 words in 45 minutes. It would take me about four or five hours if I was writing quickly. By recording, you can cut your writing time by 75%—more if you want to be precise. In this chapter we will have a look at exactly how you can achieve this outcome.

If you are an expert in your field, you can put a dollar figure on that saving. For example, say you earn $500 an hour—you will save about $1,500 per chapter on the first draft of every chapter. With nine chapters, you save yourself $13,500. Even if that time is not earning time, it's time that you could spend with your family, your friends or on sales. So it's super important.

I will show you exactly how to turn the transcript into a manuscript. In my program, a member of my team does this for you because there are a bunch of steps. However, if you haven't got that luxury, you can do this yourself. It's still much quicker than writing the chapter from scratch.

And I'll show you how to deploy an under-used superpower of your word-processing software, elements you are probably not using to their full extent. It doesn't matter if you use Word or if you use Google Docs. I'm an advocate for choosing a simple word processing software like Word or Docs rather than something complex, like Scrivener. Scrivener is a fabulous program, but it takes ages to learn. I'll show you how to make the most of the features of your chosen word processing program.

Tips for making a successful recording

Let's take it step by step. You've prepared your chapters using dot points in the Chapter Plan. Then you interview yourself. Ask yourself the question and then, through each of the points, record yourself on your phone (like me, making an idiot of yourself if anyone sees you). Perhaps you have a friend or colleague who is happy to do this with you. Just ask them to read out the questions and you talk through your answers.

Improvise your dot points a little. Imagine you are giving a talk or coaching a client, based on the notes you have in your Chapter Plan.

You would not get on stage and read out your speech. You use notes to prompt you through your points. Your chapter recordings are like that.

Recording a chapter can feel uncomfortable the first time or two. You become more fluent after recording a few chapters.

When you are ready to record your chapter, take a few breaths before you start. Talk slower than usual. Press pause for a moment if you need to collect your thoughts. That will help you stay focused. If you're working with a buddy, have a hand signal or make a request to pause when you need to. Practising for the recording can help, but it's not essential. After a few chapters, you will be comfortable and used to it.

You might say, 'But I love writing. I want to do it by writing.' Don't worry. There will be plenty of time for writing as you review and polish your chapters in the second draft, which I cover in the next chapter. Of course, if you want to write your book and you're willing to spend the extra time, you can use the Chapter Plan to do so. It'll take you three or four times as long to get your first draft down.

Your recordings will go to a transcriber so you must make them clear. Use a plug-in mike. I suggest you do a test to make sure the recording is clear. Spell out names or unusual words, such as a term you've created as part of your intellectual property, like Brain-to-Book. When you quote authors or other experts, introduce the source and their title and read the quotes verbatim (word for word), including the grammar and any tricky spelling. For example, 'Joe Pulizzi, the CEO and founder of the American Content Marketing Institute wrote in his book *Epic Content* and I quote, quote marks...' then you quote Joe verbatim and you include the full stops, the commas, the capitalisations and any quotes within the quote. When you get to the end, you say 'close quote'.

This makes your transcript more accurate and saves you the work of checking quotes at the review stage. To do this you must have them to hand when you are recording. If you plan to quote books, articles or research, which you will know because you answered question three in your Chapter Plan, mark the paragraph to quote verbatim.

Recording chapters makes your book flow. You keep momentum. I began this book in early February 2020, before the COVID19 pandemic took hold. Three or four chapters in, and the world had completely changed. I felt disorientated and distracted. Without recording my first draft, I doubt I could have written this book in the 90 days I'd set myself.

I use the American app Rev.com to transcribe my clients' recordings, but there are plenty of other suppliers including Australian ones. Whether you use Rev's transcription service or not, I suggest that you download the free Rev app. It has some useful settings, such as not closing while in use. This means you can easily see if it accidentally turns off. Many recording apps close when the screen locks.

The cost of the transcription service depends on where you are in the world. As I'm writing this book, we are in the middle of a global pandemic so the value of the Australian dollar is down at around 50 cents of the US dollar. I can't imagine why, because the US is in worse trouble than we are, but that's the situation. Perhaps you have a family member who can help you out, but transcribing is horribly hard work, and you want it back within 24 hours to keep up the momentum.

From transcript to manuscript

Now you must turn your transcript into a manuscript. It's easy, but a little tedious. But it still takes far less time than writing out the entire chapter. When you receive the transcript, it can look overwhelming. It looks nothing like a chapter in a book. Before you even start reviewing the chapter, you must follow a series of steps that transform it, or ask your virtual assistant (VA) to do these steps if you have one. If you are getting somebody else to do it, you can just photocopy or take a photo of this page.

In the early days of my program, I sent my clients the unedited transcripts, but they struggled to get them into shape. Now I provide this manuscript tune-up so, after Rev transcribes the recording, my clients see something that looks like a manuscript. It also helps that I have an editor who's terrific at this—Jess Horton of Jess Horton Creative Services. Look her up if you want somebody to do this for you. She's ace. Having someone who doesn't know about your topic do a quick review of the chapter also helps with spotting anything missing, unexplained or without a source. Jess provides that service while doing the edit and she often drops questions into the transcript. I worked with Jess on this book and her manuscript tune-up saved me so much time.

It doesn't take long to do this, but it's tedious and mechanical. Mind you, you might love having some mechanical tasks you can do in the evening or whenever you're not at the height of your creativity.

Here are the steps for your manuscript tune up:

1. **Save and name the file**
   -) Download a copy of your chapter transcript from Rev or the transcriber you're using.

   -) Upload it to Google Docs or import it into Microsoft Word—or save a copy in whichever word processing software you're using.

   -) Name the file. I suggest you use the initials of your book title, then the chapter number, then the stage of the process. For example, my book title is *Overnight Authority* and so my naming convention would be OA_Chap6_edit. Use the same naming convention for all your chapters. It'll make it a lot easier to organise all the files.

2. **Format as follows**

) **Change spacing**

Open the chapter you are working on and select all, which is usually Command-A on a Mac or ctrl-A on a PC. Make the spacing between the lines 1.5 or 2 for easier reading and reviewing. Publishers prefer double spacing.

) **Update footers and headers**

Remove any footers or headers used by the transcription services and replace with page numbers in the footers, and your name and the copyright in the header, just in case. Kath Walters © 2023.

) **Remove speakers' names with find and replace**

The keyboard shortcut for find and replace is ctrl+H in Word and Google Docs on both Mac and PC. Type in the speaker's name in Find and leave the Replace bar blank to remove. Select Replace All to remove all the names.

) **Remove tabs to align text to the left**

In the first couple of paragraphs use backspace to remove the tabs so all the text is hard left and unjustified. We only do it in a few paragraphs because I'll show you a shortcut for doing it all the way through the document using Styles.

3. **Style your text and headings**

) Select the first few paragraphs that you've formatted and go into the styles panel under the home bar. Choose 'update Normal text' to make the formatting you've done the standard. Then select the entire document and make all the text Normal.

) Open the style panel. Use Heading 1 for all the chapter titles, Heading 2 for subtopic headings and Heading 3 for headings within subtopics. You will find styles for headings down as far as you need to go.

How to make the most of the styles function

Styles is a cool and under-used feature of both Microsoft Word and Google Docs that is especially valuable for writers. You can use it to plan and review your chapter and later your manuscript.

In Microsoft Word, go to the view tab and select navigation pane. In Google Docs, click the little symbol on the top left of the page. That will open the outline view. Because you have used the style menu for the heading hierarchy, you can now see an overview of the structure of your chapter in these outline features. It's easier to spot flaws, such as gaps in information or structure that seems illogical. You can also use this to jump from section to section in your manuscript. Very helpful.

When you get to the very end of your book, you will combine all the chapters together. I'll show you how to do that later. Then you will be able to see the overview, the helicopter view of your book and its entire structure. It will, I hope, reflect the book outline you created at the start.

This can seem fiddly, but it is worthwhile. This formatting makes it easy to change the order of text, the heading structure and to find your place.

I'll leave the choice of word processing software up to you, but I have found each has one useful feature that the other does not.

Google Docs is best for collaboration. Mind you, it is the best of a bad bunch. There are few effective collaboration tools for writers on the web. Google Docs is the best I've found. The reason it is good is that it automatically saves versions of the document so you can use one version rather than saving multiple versions.

Microsoft Word's track changes feature leaves Google Docs for dead. But I am not a fan of track changes. Reading tracked copy is so difficult. For collaborating on a book, Google Docs has all but one of the features that I recommend. Where Docs falls down is the last stage of the process,

If you want to write at a gallop and speed up your first draft, record it and have it transcribed.

when you want to combine all the chapter files into a single document. To do this, you must copy and paste them.

In MS word, you can insert one document into another using the Insert File function under the Insert menu. For my money, this level of control seems much safer when you have just busted a gut for 90 days writing a book. Losing bits of text or finding your chapters are out of order is just too big a risk.

In a nutshell

If you want to write at a gallop and speed up your first draft, record it and have it transcribed. Tune up the manuscript by doing the steps I've outlined above. It's the right task for when you're not feeling creative and it's also a task to allocate to a support person such as your VA.

The styles feature of your word processing software is under-used. Now you can use it to zip around your manuscript, see an overview of the structure of each chapter, and later of the complete book. You can compare that structure with what you had originally planned in your book outline.

While recording can feel uncomfortable at first, you will take at least 75% less time to create your first draft. This makes it worthwhile.

If you do all of this to accelerate your first draft, you will have your first draft before you know it. That means it is time to polish it, just like a diamond, and make it shine.

PART THREE

Publish

BE PROUD TO SHARE YOUR
BOOK WITH THE WORLD

CHAPTER SEVEN

The Seven-Step Review

THE SHORTEST PATH TO YOUR SECOND AND FINAL DRAFT

Now you have created your first draft of your book through your recordings, you are ready to finesse and finish it. How? I have created a Seven-Step Review for you to get your draft ready to go to your first readers—people in your ideal reader group who will give you feedback (see Chapter Eight for details). This Seven-Step Review includes two steps to address your book's structure and five to address matters of style.

These seven steps will improve your book from where it is now to 80% of brilliant. But they will not make it perfect (whatever that is). There will still be room for improvement.

What do I mean by 80% of brilliant? I don't mean you leave bits out or fail to correct obvious mistakes. I don't mean you accept being sloppy. What I mean is you may not realise what the flaws of your book are until you receive some feedback. So, you do the Seven-Step Review and then seek feedback. That is what authors do.

In summary, there are two reasons why you only need to get to 80% of brilliant with the Seven-Step Review:

1. You have two more stages before you publish, and these will make your book 100% of brilliant. These stages are first-reader feedback (as mentioned above) and editing (see Chapter Nine). Both stages will radically improve the final quality of your book.

   You might wonder why you don't just press on until you hit 100% of brilliant all by yourself. The answer is that it's not possible. There is a law of diminishing returns with editing.

   The first review, using these seven steps, captures 80% of problems with your book. From there, you may improve the book each round by 5%, then 2%, then 1%. If you're a perfectionist, such reviews seem like a fabulous idea. But remember, becoming an authority means getting your book out to the readers who will be impacted and changed by it.

   With my approach, you treat your first readers and your editor as collaborators. You allow them to provide feedback and improve your book.

2. Taking this approach to reviewing your book will leave you with some 'petrol in the tank' to get you through the two final stages of publication. You are not trying to eliminate every error at this stage because you need some energy to respond to your readers and to your editor. If you try to perfect your book now, you will run out of puff. You might write (for years) until you think it's perfect and then get a soul-destroying shock when a reader points out a flaw. Instead, expect your book to need improvement at this stage.

This takes time

This is the part of writing your book that takes the most time. Applying this review may take three to four hours or even more per chapter. That is why I wanted you to create your first draft as fast as possible. Because then you have time and energy to polish it to brilliance. Most authors tackle this the other way around. They spend months, years and even decades on their first draft. Then they get some feedback about a necessary change. Ouch. They've run out of puff for polish. Result? Rough book, not polished book. You are not going to make that rookie mistake. No way.

You may feel vulnerable

You may feel vulnerable about seeking feedback from readers and from editors. I did. As I am typing these words, I am a few days from sending this book out to my first readers and I am so worried they will think it is crap. Like you, I didn't want to send anything to my readers that was less than perfect. But publishing is a process of letting go. You let go in stages. First, by sharing your ideas with me (if we work together), then with readers, then an editor, and then the world.

Perfectionism means you cannot let go. And it's just not possible to publish a book this way. It's a form of procrastination. Be brave. You are in good hands. Your readers may pick up some flaws. Be ready to have them pointed out. Feedback from me, from your readers and from your editor will make your book 100% brilliant. And the process makes you ready to send your book into the world.

Even some bestsellers are far from perfect. The late Bryce Courtenay was an advertising executive-turned-fiction-writer. His 1993 book *April Fool's Day* is among his most loved books. The story is about his son who

Perfectionism means you cannot let go. And it's just not possible to publish a book this way.

suffered from leukaemia and died from AIDS because of a transfusion. Courtenay's book is flawed, but his subject was so powerful that the book succeeded anyway.

E L James's bestseller *Fifty Shades of Gray* is another book that succeeded despite its flaws. Regardless of what you think of her topic, her book met a powerful need and made a difference in people's lives. E L James won a publishing deal even after she had published the book for free on a fan-fiction website. James became the highest-paid author in the world in 2013, with an annual income of USD95 million, according to the US business magazine *Forbes*.

Successful publication is all about mindset: the determination to put your book out there where it can have an impact. Be brave.

Prepare yourself first

Stay focused on your reader

Your book is designed to help your reader change, to have an impact and to position you as an authority. Stay focused on your reader. You know how much they need to hear your message. I bet that it is thoughts of your peers that provokes your anxiety. Try to park this. You are not writing for your peers, but for your readers (and they will love it, making your peers green with envy).

But, until you publish your book, you cannot help your reader and impact their lives.

Set yourself a deadline to complete the review of your book

Put the date in your diary. Schedule the time you need to set aside to achieve this deadline. The step after this one is to send your book to 'first readers'. More on this later.

Now prepare your book

Read a clean version through once, making no changes

The goal of the first read is to get an overall sense of the book. Print out your book, single-sided with at least 1.5 line spacing and wide margins. Read it through without making changes. Put a notepad nearby. Take notes with the page references.

If you prefer to work digitally, I suggest you upload the book into a note-taking app such as GoodNotes and make any notes in the margins. I use a digital pencil on my iPad to write my thoughts as I go, but I don't make changes to the book. Just notes.

Ignore typos and grammatical errors. These are a distraction at this stage.

As you read, consider:

) Is it clear who you wrote this book for?

) Is the overall message or purpose of the book coming across?

) Are there any parts of the book that do not support your overall purpose?

) Is the book too long?

) Is the book too short?

) Is there anything missing from the book you must include?

) Are the actions you want the reader to take clear?

Write yourself a review

When you have finished, write a page or two in your notebook in response to these questions. Try to stay out of the 'limbic' brain where you will get all flustered and hyper-critical. This is not about you, it's about your book. Keep asking yourself whether the part of the book you are reading will be valuable to your reader. Will they find it funny, useful or informative? That is really all that matters.

Fill in any gaps

If you spotted gaps during your read through, the next job is to fill them in. Is some information missing? Do you have more examples or case studies? Work out where to put them. Now add them to the manuscript.

Answer any questions

If you have worked with a coach or editor on your first draft (as happens in my Brain to Book program), answer any questions they have asked.

Use a grammar app to help you

Run your chapters through an app such as Grammarly or ProWritingAid. Buy a month of a premium subscription with Grammarly or ProWritingAid and turn on the plagiarism tracker. Put your book into the app chapter by chapter. (Neither program handles over 10,000 words at a time.)

Consider the app's recommendations. You don't have to follow them. They are especially useful for picking up passive voice. They will help you find accidental plagiarism (see Step 7 for more details). Ignore the recommendations about repetition as it applies to terminology. You must keep your terms consistent. If you are talking about leaders, don't suddenly change that term to entrepreneurs or to managers, just for variety, even if the app recommends it. But if you have repeatedly used the word 'unique', take the app's advice and think of some alternatives. (In fact, get rid of unique, unless you are talking about snowflakes.)

Then start the Seven-Step Review

Here's an overview of the Seven-Step Review before I go into more detail on each step. There are five style edits and two structural edits.

Style edits

The five style edits are:

1. Delete all words ending in 'ly.' These are adverbs. Unless they're necessary (and they almost always are not), remove 'ly' words.
2. Remove padding phrases. Don't worry—I will show you what padding phrases are.
3. Remove or explain any jargon, any acronyms and any assumed knowledge.
4. Attribute and introduce your sources.
5. Shorten all your sentences. Triple the number of full stops.

Structural edits

The two structural edits are:

6. Have you clarified your primary message for the chapter? What's the benefit to the reader of understanding your primary message? I call this the nub of your chapter or your subtopic (see Chapter Four).
7. Have you started at the exciting bit? I'll explain in more detail later in this chapter.

STEP 1) Remove all 'ly' words

Adverbs don't add to your authority. Search and destroy.

'The road to hell is paved with adverbs,' says the great American writer Stephen King. I agree. Adverbs are so seductive. They are the sirens of the writer's world, singing an irresistible melody to lure us onto the rocks and shipwreck our writing. Or, more simply, adverbs undermine the authority of your writing.

The easiest way to spot an adverb is to search for the -ly ending (it doesn't capture every adverb, but it's a splendid start). Can you find the culprit in my first paragraph now? It's the word 'simply' in my final sentence. So, what is it doing in my writing? Just what adverbs always do. An adverb is a part of speech that provides a greater description of a verb, an adjective, another adverb, a phrase, a clause, or a sentence.

The problem is not adverbs in themselves. But that adverbs proliferate. Here's King's quote in full:

> I believe the road to hell is paved with adverbs, and I will shout it
> from the rooftops. To put it another way, they're like dandelions.
> If you have one on your lawn, it looks pretty and unique. If you
> fail to root it out, however, you find five the next day... fifty the
> day after that... and then, my brothers and sisters, your lawn
> is totally, completely, and profligately covered with dandelions.
> By then you see them for the weeds they really are, but by then
> it's—GASP!!—too late.

And therein lies the problem. We use adverbs with abandon. Here's an example: 'We really love to use adverbs actually. We simply thrill to these lovely little words and the way they simply and clearly add that extra excitement and a twist to our words.' Let me write that sentence again: 'We love to use adverbs. We thrill to these words and the way they add extra excitement and a twist to our words.'

Adverbs make your writing seem breathless and exaggerated. This is not the voice of authority. How can you rid your writing of adverbs? Not in the first draft. In the first draft, fire away. Get out the adverb machine gun and spray it around. But in your second (and final) draft, search and destroy. I use the search function of Google Docs or Word and enter 'ly [space]'. That picks up most of them. Then I am ruthless. I leave only the adverbs that, when removed, make the sentence incomprehensible.

Compare a paragraph where you have searched and destroyed most adverbs. Can you see the authority shine through?

STEP 2) Remove padding phrases

Padding phrases for writers are like a runway for a plane. Writers use padding phrases to build up momentum and launch their words, just like a plane builds up momentum on the runway before it takes off. You can remove padding phrases after you're in the air.

Let me share some examples of padding phrases. Often they have personal pronouns in them, such as the sentence I wrote above, 'You can remove padding phrases after you're in the air.' 'You can' is a padding phrase. Better: 'Remove them once you're in the air.'

Some padding phrases are dangerous

Maybe. Perhaps. In my view. I think. I believe. Authors use these phrases hoping their readers will go along with their argument. Wrong. Search and remove all such phrases from your book. Why? When you write a book, you position yourself as an authority. Author. Authority. Therefore, your readers don't want to read your thought bubbles or even your beliefs. They want to read what you know.

Although such phrases of equivocation are well-intentioned, they don't help. They undermine your authority and leave the reader at sea. 'In my experience', 'research shows', 'my clients tell me', are valuable alternatives. There is the voice of authority.

You pay to edit and design every word of your book, so save yourself some money and cut out padding. Reduce your book to the leanest it can be. Readers become weary when reading unnecessary words. They drift off. They may not realise why. But they go.

Here are some examples of sentences with and without padding phrases.

With padding	Without padding
Whenever you begin to diagnose aspects of the problem you want to change, you must start with a plan.	To diagnose aspects of the problem you want to change, start with a plan.
And finally, the third complicating factor is every individual in the organisation carries a mental picture of their role and how it works or should work.	Every individual in the organisation carries a mental picture of their role and how it works or should work.
The critical factor here is people carry these preconceptions and they define their behaviour.	People carry these preconceptions and they define their behaviour.

You may worry your book will be too short if you remove all the padding. But short is fine. 'The demand for good short writing is not an innovation,' writes American author Roy Peter Craft, in his latest book *How to Write Short*. 'That need can be traced, through countless examples, back to the origins of writing itself.'

If removing the padding phrases reduces your book from 45,000 words to 25,000 words, it will be a better book. You only need as many words as it takes to explain your idea, persuade your reader you are right and then show them how to change.

Here's some tips for removing padding:

) Check all the pronouns, such as I, he, she, they, this, that and everything. Can you do without them?

) Then root out phrases like 'it's vital', 'the critical factor', 'it's important to'.

) Then search for 'that'. 'That' can almost always go.

) Now search out incorrect use of the present continuous tense and change it. For example, 'you may be starting to get excited'. Can you shorten it? For example: 'You may feel excited.' Or even, 'Excited?'

STEP 3) Remove or explain any jargon, acronyms and assumed knowledge

The art of good writing is to inform readers without making them feel silly. Jargon excludes some readers. Let me share some examples. I had been working as a journalist for a little while when an editor asked, 'When are you going to file that story?' Pre-journalism, to me filing a story would have meant putting it in the filing cabinet. But, in the world of journalism, filing a story means sending it to the editor because it's ready to go into the production process. Later, I heard an editor 'spiked' a story of mine. What on earth did spiking a story mean? This jargon comes from the past, when editors would put a story they never planned to publish on a spike sticking up on their desk. 'Spike a story' came to mean your editor won't publish your story. I didn't understand it. I wouldn't expect you to understand those pieces of jargon either. They're specific to journalism.

What about the tech term 'the cloud'? Remember when 'the cloud' entered our lexicon? Technology companies are brilliant at creating and promoting jargon. They insist everyone take it up. Heaven knows why. It took years for people to understand what 'the cloud' meant. Most people still don't. But tech people love jargon. It's a geek club and everyone is succumbing.

Many authors worry that if they don't use jargon, readers will assume they are not 'part of the club'. If I was writing a book for journalists, I might use some of that terminology to foster a feeling of inclusion. But for everyone else, I must explain it.

Remove as much jargon as you can and explain the rest. Always spell out acronyms before you use them. For example, 'What you see is what you get (WYSIWYG).' I suggest you do this at the start of each chapter. Don't assume your reader will remember the acronym from the previous chapter. If they can't remember what it means, they know they can find it earlier in the chapter they are reading.

Never assume people know any fact, even general knowledge, such as who Michelle Obama or Osama bin Laden are. Why assume? You will lose those one or two readers who do not follow politics or who were under a rock or too young on 11 September 2001. It's easy to include an explanation. It takes only seconds to write: 'The author and former first lady of the United States, Michelle Obama … ' People who know skip that information. But for people who don't know, that information informs them without making them feel stupid.

You might need to improve your jargon radar. The term 'going forward' is jargon. You don't need it. Say, 'In future,' or 'Next time,' or something simpler. I suggest before you do this review step, you have a quick squiz through *Weasel Words* by Don Watson to refresh your antenna for jargon. At the very least, take out all the obvious terms you didn't know before you entered your industry. If you're not sure whether to leave it in or leave it out, leave it out.

STEP 4) Avoid plagiarism—attribute and introduce your sources

Elegant authors quote sources and attribute ideas. People sometimes worry that if they quote other people's material they will end up undermining themselves and showing they don't have original ideas. That is a problem if you're not adding your own ideas to the debate and are over-quoting. However, clever quoting is positioning. Quoting your peers and your heroes, people you admire, is critical to positioning yourself among them and the other thought leaders in your field.

You must be polite and attribute ideas. For example, the point I made above about being the hero of your own stories is an idea I attribute to Matt Church. He was the person who shared that idea with me. I make that attribution to Matt when I talk about it with my clients and when I write about it.

Respectful authors credit the sources of their ideas and information. Proper attribution addresses your uncertainty as an author. Quoting your peers, other influential thinkers and writers positions you alongside them. It boosts your credibility. And it puts you on the moral high ground should anyone rip off your ideas and claim them as their own. After all, if you want to challenge someone who has claimed your ideas as their own, you want to point to your own book as an example of correct attribution.

Attribution is an art. Weaving in quotes and data from various sources takes a little thought, but adds richness to our writing. That makes it worth the effort. How do you do it? Do you include reference notes at the bottom of the page? Academic writing contains references and footnotes. You can do this through Microsoft Word. But this is a business book, so don't include footnotes. References at the bottom can distract and suggest your book is a textbook rather than a business book. (If you feel the need to direct people to further reading, provide a 'further reading' list either at the end of the book or chapter.)

Quoting is difficult to do elegantly. Too much attribution is laborious to read. Too little is rude and may border on plagiarism. These are not the qualities you want in your writing. You want memorable, inspiring and thought-provoking.

'If I have seen further, it is by standing on the shoulders of giants,' English physicist and mathematician Sir Isaac Newton wrote in a letter to his brother in 1676. Newton's way of expressing humility and gratitude was so 'sticky' it has stayed with us for over 300 years! But let's not scare ourselves with such lofty standards. You need not be as poetic as Newton.

Skilful attribution is learnable. In fact, you do it all the time. 'Guess what Jane told me last Friday night,' you may say over coffee with a buddy. Or, 'Kath Walters' writing about plagiarism is so useful,' you might write on Facebook or Twitter and share a link to this book (just kidding ... or not).

Here are some simple principles to help you avoid the pitfalls of plagiarism and respect your sources.

Get their name, title and biographical details right

When I quoted Newton, I wrote that he was a scientist. But I wasn't sure exactly when he lived, so I went to several sources: Wikipedia, which I am not snobby about, the Encyclopaedia Britannica, and Biography.com. I found Newton variously described as a mathematician, astronomer, philosopher and physicist.

Then I checked the British broadcaster, the BBC, a source I trust. I discovered Newton wasn't such a pleasant guy. Despite his memorable quote, Newton's story 'is also one of a monstrous ego who believed that he alone was able to understand God's creation. His private life was far from rational: consumed by petty jealousies, bitter rivalries and a ruthless quest for reputation,' according to BBC.co.uk. But the BBC called him a physicist and mathematician so I went with that.

It's always worth checking! He was knighted in April 1705 and so I must correctly title him *Sir* Isaac Newton.

Start with the quote, then attribute the source (with one exception)

The website The Writer's Handbook has this advice:

> Integrating a quotation into your text usually involves two elements:
>
> 1. A signal that a quotation is coming—the author's name and/or a reference to the work
>
> 2. An assertion that indicates the relationship of the quotation to your text.

I disagree. Put the quote first. Who you are quoting is less exciting than what they say unless you are quoting a global celebrity who is not very interesting. Newton's quote comes first, and then I name my source. Start at the most exciting part of your idea in every chapter, subtopic, paragraph, sentence and quote.

There is an exception to this rule. When you switch sources, introduce the source first to avoid confusion about who is saying what. But make your introduction as short as possible.

Seek permission

The rules of copyright are quite complex and they vary around the world. I am not a copyright lawyer and you cannot use the following advice to defend a breach. That said, here are the principles.

Everything you write is immediately copyright to you, whether or not you apply the © symbol on your work (a good idea). You do not have to pay for your own copyright (so watch the scammers). It lasts for a period of time, such as 50 years, variable by jurisdiction. If you want to quote someone else and the material is under copyright, you must ask permission, except for 'fair dealing'. I have two suggestions here:

1. If in doubt, ask for permission. This means contacting the author and providing them with the exact quote you want to use and requesting permission. It's polite to do so. (And you might make a new friend. I did.) If you can't get in touch with them, ask their publisher. The copyright holder may request a fee. That is their right. Then you can decide whether to use the quote. Mention the likely print quantity of the first edition. The lower the quantity, the less expensive (or likely) the fee.

2. Go to a reliable source, such as a copyright lawyer or a reputable organisation, to find out more information. In Australia, The Australian Copyright Council is one such organisation (copyright.org.au). Beware of the scam sites.

Perform a plagiarism check with an app

Sometimes you may plagiarise without being aware of it. You use an expression only to discover it deserves attribution. Did you know that a woman called Patty Hill held the copyright to the song 'Happy Birthday' in the European Union until 2017, for example? It's easy to make a mistake.

Imagine if you could press a button and discover ideas or phrases that breach copyright rules. Well, you can. The plagiarism option of spelling and grammar apps, such as Grammarly and ProWritingAid, offers an option that checks your text against 'billions of web pages' (they say) if you lash out and pay for the premium version. Not only does this feature alert you about possible breaches, it shows you the source. Now you can attribute it. Yay.

STEP 5) Triple your full stops. Shorten every sentence

My favourite book about writing is *Write Like Hemingway*. Its author, Dr R Andrew Wilson, shares his love for the great American fiction writer by unpacking all that is elegant, lean and learnable from Hemingway's books.

Hemingway was the master of the concise sentence. He understood the power of brevity. The stronger your point, the fewer words you need to make it. Hemingway changed journalism and fiction with his succinct writing style.

When you shorten your sentences, the meaning or the lack of meaning becomes clear. If your point is confusing, shortening your sentence makes it obvious. It's also great for building pace or rhythm in your writing—an overlooked quality. Not that every sentence you write should be a short one; you would end up sounding like a telegram.

As a writer, harness the rhythm of words and change the pace for your readers.

You might say, 'I can't do it. I've tried to shorten my sentences and I can't triple the number of full stops.' Yes. You. Can. Keep at it. Restructure your sentences. They will be easier to understand if you shorten them.

There are no exceptions to this rule. If everyone did this, the world of words would be like the Kyoto Botanical Gardens in the cherry blossom season—stunning.

When you do this step, work fresh. This is a demanding task. Work in sprints—25 minutes of sentence shortening, then a five-minute break. Get up, walk around, do a little dance, then sit back down and do another sprint. Remember, vary the pace. Don't make every sentence short. Let some flow happen. It'll develop a nice pace in your writing. You might wonder whether it's worth the effort. Yes, it is. This step and Step Seven—starting at the exciting bit—are the two most powerful in the Seven-Step Review.

STEP 6 ⟩ Clarify your point

In 1990, Elizabeth Newton earned a PhD in psychology at Stanford University by studying a simple game in which she assigned people one of two roles: 'tappers' or 'listeners'. In this experiment, Newton showed that people assume their listeners can understand them. She asked the tappers in this experiment to tap out the rhythm of a well-known song, such as 'Happy Birthday'. The tapper chose from a list of 25 common songs. The listener had to guess what the tune was. How often do you think they guessed correctly? Most of us would expect the listeners to guess the right answer.

But that wasn't the reality. Out of the 120 songs tapped in Newton's experiment, listeners guessed only 2.5% of the songs. Three songs out of 120. This is astonishing. But even more surprising was the fact the tappers predicted 50% of the listeners would guess the song. The tappers were wildly optimistic about how well the listeners could understand their tapping. This applies to writers too. You may assume readers understand your message as you intend it. But this happens much less often than you realise.

Have you made the primary messages for every chapter, paragraph, subtopic and sentence clear? Your writing will stand out from the crowd if you address this point. Spell out your message to make sure you get it across.

Writers may worry about patronising the reader by doing this. If you notice your writing drifting into a patronising tone, use more stories. Using more stories builds more empathy with the reader and shows you understand them. Describe what might be difficult for them to understand.

Don't overuse the pronoun 'we' to convey empathy. That sounds patronising. It's a shortcut to sounding empathetic that can backfire. Readers bristle when they don't have the choice to include themselves.

So, instead of, 'We writers make a mistake in assuming the person who's reading our book agrees with us,' Instead, try: 'Writers commonly make this mistake'. Leave room for your reader to choose whether your primary message includes them.

Make sure you have included the nub, too. Convey why your message is important and how it benefits the reader. What does your reader risk if they don't understand your point? Remove everything from your book that does not benefit the reader. Every chapter. Every subtopic. Every paragraph. Every sentence. Every word.

Consider each chapter and ask yourself, 'Is the primary message of my chapter clear? Have I spelled out the message and the point at the end of the story I've told? Is the message of each subtopic clear? Could each subtopic be a blog on its own?' By asking yourself these questions, you will quickly understand whether you're making the point you want to make, while also providing reasons for the reader to believe you.

STEP 7) Start at the exciting bit

Start at the exciting bit of each chapter, subtopic, paragraph, sentence. More often than not, the most exciting bit is a story, but it might also be a big number or a shocking statistic.

I'm standing on a train station platform and the train is going past me. There is a passenger on the train 20 metres to my left. They have not yet passed me. There's also a passenger 20 metres on my right, towards the front of the train who has just passed me. At that moment, I am a living example of Einstein's space-time continuum. The BBC used this story to explain Einstein's theory of relativity and its relationship to time in its series on free will. If they had started their video by saying, 'Now, let me explain the space-time continuum of the magnificent professor Albert Einstein,' I would have already drifted off or perhaps gone to watch some Nordic detective series on Netflix.

Consider each chapter and ask yourself, 'Is the primary message of my chapter clear? Have I spelled out the message and the point at the end of the story I've told? Is the message of each subtopic clear? Could each subtopic be a blog on its own?'

When you start at the exciting bit, you snag the reader's attention away from the demands of the everyday. You hold them in suspense. Human minds are prediction machines. If your reader can predict the end of your sentence or paragraph, what might they do?

You guessed it. They skip it.

The BBC used this vivid story to hold my attention until I understood the point they were making. That image of me on the station, with the person 20 metres ahead and the person 20 metres behind has stuck in my mind. I can now explain one of the most complex concepts in physics. It's memorable, or as Chip and Dan Heath, authors of *Make it Stick*, would say, 'it's sticky'. You want as much stickiness as possible in everything you write.

Most writers start with the background before they write about the exciting bit. They worry that if they launch into the most exciting statement or story, the reader won't understand what they are talking about. The opposite is true. Your reader is more interested in learning what you are talking about once they've become hooked by your story. The train station story is an example. I'm not interested in Albert Einstein's theory of relativity and the space-time continuum until I have a relatable picture in my mind. My struggle to understand the example only makes me more interested.

First, check out your stories. Could you bring the stories or perhaps even some fascinating data up to the top of your chapter or subtopic?

When I first wrote this step (seven), I started with my main message, and why it matters and all my other advice. When I edited this step, I moved the story of the train station close to the top because I wanted to snag your attention. Stories are one way to hook your readers' attention. Another way is to find the part of the chapter or subtopic that makes *you* excited. Can you start there?

Make sure you use this principle when you quote sources. Start with the interesting quote before you introduce the source. Even if they're a Harvard professor. Their status as a Harvard professor is an important credibility booster, but readers don't care unless they find the quote valuable and interesting. The credential supports the statement, not the other way around.

You might worry that you'll lose the structure of your chapter with so many changes. That is a risk. As you move things around, you may lose links between the points you made when you recorded this chapter. Work systematically to avoid this. The way I do this is to think about the big sections of the chapter and then the small sections of each big section. Helpful, eh? Let me explain.

The big sections of a chapter are as follows. Each chapter has an introduction and a conclusion. Between them are three to seven (or more) subtopics. You can tell where a subtopic is because it will have a subheading. So your chapter looks like this, for example:

-) Introduction
-) Subtopic 1
-) Subtopic 2
-) Subtopic 3
-) Conclusion

In each of those big sections there are four small sections and they are moveable.

-) **The main message:** What you are talking about.
-) **The nub or why section:** Why your message matters to the reader.
-) **The story or evidence:** How you prove you are right about your message.
-) **The action:** How your reader can use what you say.

So, in each of the big sections, can you move the small sections around? Could you start your introduction with a story, or even with the nub? Could you start it with an action? I started my introduction with a story about the sabre-tooth tiger. I started Chapter Three with a story about Picasso. But with Chapter One, I led with my main message.

You don't have to go crazy with changing things around. Just mix up the structure a bit to keep the readers on their toes, and tweak their interest.

In a nutshell

If you use these seven steps, you will improve your book to 80% of brilliant. These steps will help you improve every piece of writing you undertake—every blog, every email. Use them all the time.

You might say, 'Hey, it won't make my writing perfect.' But remember the law of diminishing returns. This will give you an enormous improvement. The next round might give you a 10% improvement, then 5% and then 1%. Meanwhile, your book is not out helping the people you want to help. And remember, you want to save some fuel in your tank for the feedback from readers and from your editor. Do these seven steps knowing your book won't be perfect (no matter what you do) and you'll have the energy to take on feedback from your first readers and your editor.

Work systematically through your first draft, chapter by chapter, and apply these steps. This may take three to four hours per chapter.

Now, you are ready for a remarkable moment. In Chapter Eight, you will take a step towards sharing your book with the world. First stop? Your target audience. I'll guide you through getting feedback from your first readers. They will help you let your book go, so you can publish it and serve your readers and the world. *Cool!*

Test with Your Target Audience

HOW TO ASK FOR FEEDBACK AND
RECEIVE THE BEST KIND

I live in a block of nine flats in Maribyrnong, in Melbourne's west. I bought this flat in 2010 (there is a point to this story), but I moved out for five years (long story). One of my neighbours, Chris, was writing his book when I moved in. When I moved out, Chris was still writing his book. The same one. Not good. I don't want you to be that guy. (Sorry, Chris.) I want you to finish your book. I want you to get your book out there and overcome the natural fear of getting your book to your target reader.

The first step to finishing your manuscript is to overcome your fears. If you don't, you'll join the 97% club who wrote their book and filed it in the top drawer of their desk. You want to be in the 3% club who write and publish their books.

In this chapter you will learn how to publish your book. It is a process of letting go. This starts with what I call 'first readers'. I will show you how to find them and make the most of their help. In the next chapter, you'll learn how to choose an editor and designer and get your book out into the world. These are the steps involved in publishing and letting go of your book. Let me first start with some important points about letting go.

First, you must solve Buddha's last challenge: self-doubt. I'll share some secrets about befriending the inner demon of doubt, not crushing it. Second, you'll learn about one principle of letting go, which is to identify the common trigger for your fears—imagining your peers picking up your book and having a good old laugh and gossip behind your back. It's an awful image. I'm imagining it right now. It's like being dunked in a barrel of ice-cold water repeatedly. You'll learn to shift your focus from your peers and reboot your courage to put your book out there.

Buddha's last challenge: taming the inner demon

In ancient India, five centuries BC, Buddha sat under the Bodhi tree, determined to sit there until he achieved enlightenment. Under the tree, Buddha encountered all the shadow energies brought to him by the god Mara, the god of the shadow side. Through the night, Buddha met Mara's challenges of greed, hatred and delusion with mindful awareness and compassion. The story goes that each of the negative energies, as they met the Buddha, transformed into flowers. When the morning star rose in the sky, heaps of flowers lay at the feet of the Buddha.

In the last moments before Buddha's transformation, Mara threw down his ultimate challenge. 'Who do you think you are to assume the seat of a Buddha?' asked Mara. 'Who are you to assume the capacity for an awakened heart and mind?' He planted the seed of doubt.

As you quake with the possibility that your book is unworthy, you are in excellent company. And the solution to the challenge that I present to you here is the same approach that Siddhartha Gautama adopted in the moments before he overcame the last challenge and achieved enlightenment and became Buddha.

You may not achieve enlightenment, but you will publish your book

We all have an inner critic: the voice inside our head that comments on our every thought and action. Typically, the inner critic is not very kind to us. Psychologists suggest the inner critic's voice reflects the stories we have internalised from our childhood when an adult delivered some guidance with too much force, too little care, or passed on their own negative beliefs without even being aware of them.

When you sit down to write, that inner critic can transform into an inner demon: a critic so vicious that you cannot get a word written. As soon as you put down a word, the inner demon is there to taunt you and you hastily scratch your pen through your words or delete them from your laptops or iPads completely. And you are back to the empty page. Here are some typical comments of my inner demon:

) That's rubbish.
) A two-year-old could write better than you.
) If your clients see that, they will sack you on the spot.
) Start again.
) Is that what you call original?

Yeah, my demon is ugly. But you get the picture.

Don't slay the demon

Your goal as a writer is to make sure the inner critic does not overpower you and bring your writing to a halt. Although we battle the demon at every stage of writing, I have noticed it becomes overpowering towards the end. As the moment of going public (publishing) draws closer, our doubts can seem overwhelming.

Many writing teachers will tell you to silence the inner voice and suggest ways to do it. Writing in the *Huffington Post*, coach and author

Marcia Sirota likens the inner critic to an abusive partner and advises us to get rid of it.

I advise you to follow the Buddha's wisdom. Faced with Mara's humiliating challenges to his worthiness, the Buddha responded by inviting Mara to tea. In the ancient story, the Buddha's response caused Mara to disappear in the puff of smoke.

But, since you are not enlightened yet, do not expect Mara to vanish. Calm the doubt. You don't want your inner critic to abuse you or paralyse you. And then start a dialogue with the demon.

Why? The inner critic can be the voice of your reader, asking valid questions about the readability of what you are writing. This is a daring strategy, but you can harness your inner demon to help you identify what is good and what is bad in your writing and help you review and edit your work. It is all a matter of how you bring the inner critic into the writing process.

How to turn the inner critic into Mummy's little helper

The inner critic is not such a bad ol' fellow. She (or he) just takes herself a little too seriously and is way too eager to get involved. Your job is not to get rid of her; it is to help the inner critic find her place in the writing process.

The inner critic is not helpful early on when writing your first draft. This is when she can do the most damage. She stops us from getting our words written at all. Here are some strategies to tame the inner critic and put her in her place.

Outrun her

The inner critic wants to slow everything down. One of the easier ways to put her in her place is to outrun her when you are writing your first draft. By this I mean write quickly without stopping. If you are typing, no deleting. If you are handwriting, no crossing out. If you are recording, no stopping. Just keep going.

When doubts arise, promise your inner critic you will give her a little more involvement in the writing process. But only when you come to the end of your first draft.

Give her the floor

The inner critic is like Shakespeare's shrew (*The Taming of the Shrew.*) She's sparky, witty and wild. You want to harness her energy but not let her run the show. But you can sometimes give her the floor. When your inner critic is madly dancing, write whatever she tells you to write.

When you write a sentence and the inner critic tells you it's crap, write that down. For example: 'Ok, this book is actually crap and I sometimes feel I cannot write a word that is not crap.' Then move on to the next sentence. This might seem a little cumbersome, but at least you can keep moving. Later, you might edit her out. But not always. See below.

Listen to her advice

Once you have finished the first draft, you are ready to apply some critical faculties to your work. The inner critic can be helpful. If you have made a note of her nasty comments as you were writing, have a read before you delete everything she says. She might have a point. Perhaps your inner critic is channelling what a sceptical reader might think when they read your work.

For example, as you read my words in the previous point you may think: 'Really? You want me to waste time writing nasty comments about my writing. I mean, how much of a waste of time is that? And what a negative experience!'

And I may include that comment in this chapter (which I have in a nifty little way) and answer it. My answer is that it's better to stand up

Keep dialogues with your inner critic short and infrequent. The inner voice grows big and hairy if you give her too much oxygen. Put her in her place, don't give her a job as CEO.

from the desk with words on the paper—even if they are nasty words—rather than no words. And when you write down what the inner critic says, without taking her too seriously, her words can end up in your story and make it better.

Have a chat with her

Some years ago, one of my clients read me an entertaining dialogue between him and his inner critic. He wrote it beautifully and sincerely. In this dialogue with his critic, he discovered much about himself, his writing and the purpose of his work as he wrote.

To make any dialogue with your inner voice valuable, write it down. When you argue with the inner voice in your head, you lose. The result? You get nothing done. And insist that she improves her manners. Our inner critics tend to be cruel. If that is the case, don't listen. Just say, 'Talk to the hand, inner critic!' until she can say something constructive. Don't let her abuse you. Let her express specific doubts about your writing.

Keep dialogues with your inner critic short and infrequent. The inner voice grows big and hairy if you give her too much oxygen. Put her in her place, don't give her a job as CEO.

Give your inner critic a role (in the chorus)

Make like the Buddha and invite your inner demon to tea. Give her a role, but put her in the chorus. Your inner critic wants to be a star. She wants to have the floor all the time; she needs to know when it's her turn to speak. She wants to be rude. Don't let her be. Give her a role. Her role is to come in after the first draft and help you see your writing as others would perceive it. Invite her in when she can help. Let her know when you need her. And when you do not. When you practise befriending your inner critic, you will gain confidence. Few real critics are as tough as we are on ourselves.

There is a common trigger for an out-of-control critic, and once you know about it, you are more likely to bring her under control.

You're not writing for your peers

Use the reader you imagined in Chapter One to help you edit your book, then send it out for editing and for reviewing by first readers. Remembering to shift your focus back to your reader will give you the courage to move and put it out there.

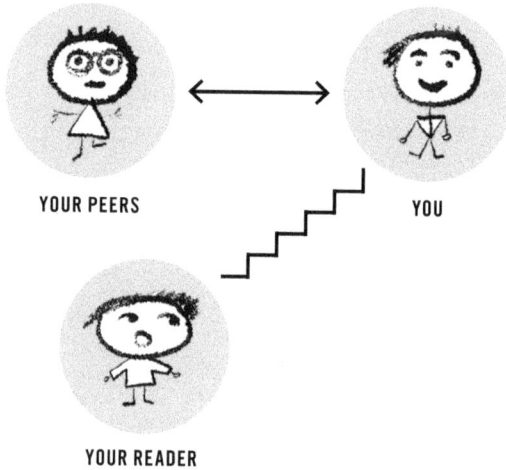

YOUR PEERS

YOU

YOUR READER

Illustration: Kath Walters

You and your peers are at the top level of this diagram. Your readers are several levels down. I am not disparaging your readers. They have areas of expertise that you don't have. But in your field of expertise, your readers will be several levels below you. Your job is to bring them up to your level as they read your book.

Our egos, as writers and even as human beings, are fragile. If this is your first book, it'll be even more fragile. The closer you get to publishing, the more vulnerable you will feel. It's easy to default to serving your ego and impressing your peers instead of serving your reader at this point in the book writing process.

I've seen it with my clients. They become clear in the early stages about their reader. The closer they get to publication, the more they admit to me they're thinking about their peers judging their work. To be honest, I feel it myself. Here I am, on the couch on a rainy Saturday, writing my book. It's for you, dear reader. You want my guidance, I am sure. And yet I'm afraid of my heroes and my peers judging this book and pointing to its flaws. I'm sure there are many ways my book could improve. But that's about my ego. If I put it aside and remind myself that I want to serve you, dear reader, my ego settles. I want to help you get your book out into the world, where it can help change the world.

My client Annie Sheehan mastered this moment. Her book, *The Courageous Sponsor,* is about project management and the role of the sponsor in championing projects to a successful conclusion. She is brilliant at identifying the pitfalls many sponsors fall into and has terrific techniques to guide them through those moments. She developed these skills over her 20-plus years in the project management and project sponsorship field.

At the end of 2019, she was coming to the end of writing the book. She was at the Project Management Institute and mentioned her book to a friend there. 'Oh,' he said, 'you're one of all those project managers who writes a book for project managers about project management.'

Annie came back to him without a second's hesitation, 'No, my book is for sponsors of projects, helping them to do a better job as they sponsor projects from idea to a successful conclusion.' Her colleague was both humbled and astonished. He immediately grasped the value of such a book and said, 'That's fantastic. I can't wait to read it.' His scepticism turned to admiration in a moment. Annie achieved that personal moment of triumph because she was crystal clear about her readership and had been from the word go.

Hang on, I hear you plead. 'I'm trying to write a book that builds my authority. If I don't pitch it at my peers, won't I look stupid and undermine my authority?' Think of Annie. Would her book be of any value to her peers? No, it was for the readers who needed it to succeed.

You must build your authority with your market. You show your authority with what you say—your intelligent content, and what you do—serving your readers. Be seen as the leader by the people you serve. Even as I make this claim, I quake in my boots. I think of people I admire:

>) Ann Handley, author of *Everybody Writes*
>) Joe Pulizzi, the founder of the Content Marketing Institute
>) Seth Godin, the thought leader in 'permission marketing' and author of many books including *Purple Cow*.

But my book is not for my heroes, as much as I'd love them to admire it. My book is for you. If you write your book for your peers, it's a textbook. It is not a business book.

How to review with your readers in mind

Go back to your Ultimate Guide to Getting Your Book Started and refresh your memory about all the points that you made there: what you're trying to achieve, who you're writing for, what their problems are, what the causes of those problems are, what the impact of those problems are. You have the fate of your readers in your hands. Please take that responsibility seriously. Get back in tune with your motivations for writing this book.

As you go through your book—every chapter, every subtopic, every paragraph and every sentence—ask yourself, 'Would my reader find this useful? Could I make this sentence, paragraph, chapter, subtopic more useful to my reader?'

I have a reader in mind as I write this book. Of course I do. The person I have in mind stands in for all of you wonderful people.

There's only one barrier to doing this: fear. Courage is not the absence of fear. To be courageous is to 'Feel fear and do it anyway', as the wonderful Susan Jeffers wrote decades ago. Feel that fear, as I do, of your peers and your heroes judging your work, and set it aside. Don't quash it or eliminate it. Just set it aside in service of your reader.

The role of your first readers

The next step toward publication is to share your book with what I call 'first readers'. In the next chapter, I'll talk about editors. After that, you're ready to go to the world. For now, let's have a look at your first readers.

A first reader is what it sounds like: the first person who reads your manuscript. Get their feedback and incorporate their suggestions before you send your manuscript to your editor. If you do this *after* you have your manuscript edited, your editing costs increase.

Choose first readers in your target market. That way you can test your book and invite a response from the people you hope to reach. Also, choose people who would like you to succeed: your supporters, clients or colleagues.

If you don't approach first readers, there are two potential risks. One is ending up in a loop of perfecting your manuscript, trying to imagine the reader's feedback and correcting it. The other is that you miss the mark. Every book is a best guess. Yours is an expert guess based on your experience. But it is still a guess. You're about to test your guess.

The analogy here is using an 'agile' process in software development. Developers talk about creating a 'minimum viable product', getting the target market to try it out, collating their responses, and incorporating that feedback into their software. You will do exactly that with your second draft.

Grace Lever, an Australian digital marketing expert and the founder of many successful digital marketing projects, including the Do-ers Inner

Circle, has a phrase I love—'Doers take massive imperfect action'. Take the massive imperfect action. It is a massive action to write a book. It will be imperfect. It cannot be perfect because you are not perfect. We are human.

How to get the most from first readers

The best way to approach first readers is in a way that is both respectful and will elicit the most useful feedback. Clients often ask me, 'Should I send it to an editor first?' The answer is no because you haven't finished writing your book yet. You are in the last stage of reviewing it. You need the feedback from these readers first.

Here's the process:

〉 Choose two or three people who you trust and whose opinion you value and ask them to read it (voluntarily).

〉 Give them at least two or three weeks' notice before you plan to send them your manuscript. Give them two weeks to review the manuscript after checking if that is ok with them.

〉 If you cannot make the agreed deadline, let them know as early as possible. Try hard to hit it, even if it means working all night.

〉 Make sure you format your manuscript consistently. Use at least 1.5 line spacing. Make sure the left margin is wide so if they print it, there is enough room for them to write comments.

〉 Remind them about the deadline as negotiated when you approached them.

〉 Be clear about the feedback you want from your readers. It makes their job easier. It gives them a structure to work with and helps them help you.

I suggest asking your readers at least the following questions:

) Are you clear who this book is for?

) Is the overall message or purpose of the book clear?

) Are there any parts of the book that do not support my overall message?

) Is any part of the book too long?

) Is any part of the book too short?

) Is there anything missing from the book that you would love to see included?

) Are you clear about what action I want the reader to take because of reading this book?

) If you liked this book, would you write a two- or three-line testimonial about what you liked? If so, may I use the quote on the printed cover design or inside the book?

Ask extra questions that matter to you. A friend of mine had a great additional question:

) How could I make my book funnier?

You'll note the last question in my list is to request a testimonial for the book. I suggest you also request a testimonial from one of your heroes.

And finally, when you get your reader's feedback, say thank you, and add them to the acknowledgements section. Promise them a free copy of your book and give them two.

How to respond to first-reader feedback

Feedback is helpful, but we have a choice about whether we respond to it. Think through the responses you have received before changing your manuscript. Make a list of the feedback or comments that you want to respond to. If you are not sure about any point of feedback, write it down on the list and then go back to it. Ask yourself: If I respond to this feedback, will it make this book more helpful to my audience? Then go through your draft and make all the changes on your list.

Your first readers may come back and say stuff that you don't like, that you don't think is helpful, or that doesn't advance the project. Let me assure you, not all feedback is right. But please get feedback and consider it. Also, this is unlikely. Your first readers are on your side.

Appoint a champion

Before I finish this chapter, I want to pass on some advice from Genevieve Hawkins, author of *Mentally at Work*. Appoint a champion who will hold you to your goal of publishing when your will wavers. For me, it was my writing group. For Genevieve, it was her sister, Leonie Green, author of *Stop Doubting, Start Leading*. This is sage advice. A champion will push you, if you let them, over the line of self-doubt into the zone of service.

In a nutshell

Publishing is letting go. Each of the last three chapters in this book— the Seven-Step Review, testing with first readers, and in the next chapter, working with your editor—takes you closer to letting go of your manuscript and sharing it with the world. It toughens you up a little by exposing your vulnerability to the world, one step at a time.

Like a chick in an egg—first, it has the large barrier of the eggshell. When the chick grows a little—not when it's ready to fly, but when it's ready to eat a little food—it pecks open the egg and hops out into the world. Gradually, its feathers form and it flies and thrives in the world on its own. That's publishing for you. It's a process of gradually removing protections and, once you've pecked open the shell, making sure you can thrive in the world as an author.

You've learned the three most important aspects of the letting go process. The first is to tame the inner demon and face, as Buddha did, the last challenge—self-doubt. You've learned to remind yourself of the person you are writing for (and ignoring your peers) to overcome perfectionism. And you have learned to let go by sending your manuscript to first readers to elicit valuable feedback.

Don't join the 97%-club—all those authors who have their book manuscripts in their top drawer and have never published them. You are a thought leader. Be in the 3%-club. You are so close. You are nearly there. Keep going. Don't give up. 'Feel the fear and do it, anyway.'

In Chapter Nine, you will learn the ultimate steps to publication. You'll discover how to decide whether traditional publishing or self-publishing is best for you. I will show you how to choose an editor who's right for you. They're not all born equal. And you will learn the principles of brilliant book design and how to get your book printed. It's very simple. Keep going.

CHAPTER NINE

Get Published

ONLY BY PUBLISHING CAN YOU CLAIM YOUR AUTHORITY

When you're an authority, clients come to you. Think about it. People want to be associated with authors. Why? For good reason. The moment you publish is the moment you move from expert to authority. Overnight.

You deserve this. You have done the hard work. No matter how systematic you are, it's not easy to write a book. You deserve the authority you are about to command by publishing your book. It's a huge accomplishment to write a book.

Now you have written, reviewed and tested your book, the process from here might be summarised with this diagram:

EDITING   DESIGN

1   2   3   4   AUTHORITY

         PROOFREADING   PRINTING

These last four topics take you all the way to publication. Yay. I am already excited for you.

First I will help you explore the choice between traditional and self-publishing. Which one is right for you? Next, I guide you through the process of choosing an editor. Not all editors are born equal so you must choose with care. After that, I'll cover the three principles of great book design. Finally, I'll show you how to get your book printed. Print-on-demand has made self-publishing possible. So here you are. You're within a stone's throw of the end of your book journey.

When, why and how to approach a 'traditional' publisher with your business book manuscript

One of the most common questions I am asked by my clients is, 'How do I get a book deal?' or, 'How can I get 'traditional publishers' to publish my book?'

Since I began my Brain to Book in 90 Days program, I have helped authors win global publishing deals with traditional publishers. Which is pretty self-sacrificing of me, since I'm an advocate of indie authors—the self-publishing model.

I am not going to try to dissuade you from approaching traditional publishers; I am going to discuss when, why and how to win the interest of a traditional publisher. (From here on, I am calling them publishers, not traditional publishers.)

What is a publisher?

Publishers are in the business of finding authors who will write a book for them, and then editing, designing, printing, marketing and distributing that book to bookshops for sale. Publishers make money by sharing the profits (money made after costs are deducted) from the book sales with authors.

Typically, publishers do not pay authors to write unless they can guarantee a large return, meaning lots of book sales. In this case they may pay 'an advance'. Publishers look for books with a mass appeal rather than a niche interest, especially those with global markets because Australia has such a small population. That said, most publishers have a speciality: business, cooking, travel, fiction, etc.

Today, the publishing model is being disrupted. Many publishers are demanding more from authors and providing less. I'll explain a bit more about this later.

Why approach a publisher?

The most common reason authors want publishers, rather than choosing indie- or self-publishing, is for 'third-party endorsement': the prestige of your manuscript being chosen from among the many submitted to them. I have arguments against the value of this in today's market, but that is not what this chapter is about—you do win prestige in the eyes of the market when a respected publisher takes on your book.

However, remember that it is only worth approaching a publisher if your book has mass appeal: publishers cannot make money unless they sell a lot of your books.

What you get from the deal

In addition to the status of third-party endorsement, a publisher will assign a good editor and an experienced book designer to your book, and pay for printing and distribution. These services are worth many thousands of dollars, so it's a great deal for you. This means publishers share the risk—the upfront costs before any returns from sales—of publishing your book.

Today, the publishing model is being disrupted. Many publishers are demanding more from authors and providing less.

What you don't get

Today, publishers often demand that you share the financial risk by insisting that you buy a minimum quantity of your own book at a reduced rate, from a couple of hundred to many thousands, in order to 'seed the market' with free copies. In short, authors today pay some of the editing, design and printing costs.

Publishers used to help a lot with marketing and media promotion, but this has changed. Although authors have always had to work hard to promote their books, doing speaking gigs, radio and TV appearances, publishers used to help more. Today, many authors have to employ their own publicists at a cost of several thousands of dollars.

How to approach a publisher

There are a couple of absolute clangers that mark you out as an amateur in the way you approach a publisher. While it's fair enough that you aren't an expert, you are negotiating a commercial deal, so you want to wise up to get the best one you can.

1. Don't lob your whole manuscript to a publisher

Approach them in the early stages of writing your book when you have a title, a book outline and one or two chapters written. Why? Because you will get a faster response. Also, you are more likely to get a yes or a maybe, rather than a flat no. That's because they can have some influence over the direction of your manuscript. If you have written a book called How to Halve Your Weekly Food Bill, they might make a small suggestion, such as How to Halve Your Weekly Food Bill in Six Easy Steps. They are providing a commercial insight that might improve your book sales. However, responding to that may radically alter your approach to writing the book.

2. Follow their submissions guidelines

Almost every publisher today provides resources to authors that guide their submissions. Annoyingly, they are all slightly, but not significantly, different. You are going to have a better chance of winning their attention if you show that you have done a bit of your own research and discovered that they have a process you can follow.

3. The fortune is in the follow-up

The world's best sales trainer, Rachel Bourke, founder of SalesSPACE, has a favourite saying: 'The fortune is in the follow-up'. Same goes if you want to win a publishing deal. Don't sit around waiting for your rejection slip; get on the phone and use your winning ways to secure the deal. Start by saying you are calling to ensure they received your proposal. Ask the name of the person who is reviewing it (although it's best to know this before you send it). Ask to speak to that person and see if they need further information, have any reservations, etc. Publishers look for energetic, confident authors who believe in the value of their work. Be that author.

10 fabulous reasons to self-publish your book

Now that I have shared tips on how to win a publishing deal, I can in good conscience share with you 10 reasons you shouldn't bother.

Self-publishing makes more sense financially and strategically if you are an expert and you want to share your message with the world. So, let's hit the ground running with all 10 reasons right up front and then I'll take you through the number one reason in detail. The rest of this chapter is about how to do it.

1. Gives fastest return on investment (see detail below).
2. Takes less time. Most publishers take nine months to one year to get your book to market.

3. Is cheaper than some 'traditional' deals. Publishers may contract you to buy back your books, covering their costs.

4. Focuses on the right metrics. Your book sells you and your ideas.

5. Simplifies your marketing strategy. You use your book to increase your credibility, open doors and stay ahead of the competition. It's that simple.

6. Increases (rather than decreases) returns over time. The cost in time and money is at the start. But a book will last you three to five years as a marketing tool, possibly a lifetime.

7. Retains control over editing, design and print quality.

8. Reduces waste and costs. Why print 1000 or 5000 copies when 200 will achieve your goals?

9. Is still possible to get a distribution deal (if you get an ISBN).

10. Might open the door to a publishing deal later if you have written a bestseller (a marked change in attitude on the part of traditional publishers).

The fastest return on investment (ROI)

Self-publishing delivers the fastest ROI of time and money that you spend on your book. This is the absolute fundamental of the business-book strategy. See the graphic on the next page. It's a visual short-cut of the explanation.

Let me take you through it.

Let's say, for argument, your speaker fee or coaching program is worth $5000. (Hey, if it's less than that, put your prices up).

You publish your book and it helps you sell an additional four keynotes or programs. Now you have paid for all the costs associated with self-publishing your book (let's say $19,000, but you can do it for less).

Every program you sell from then on is profit on this marketing strategy. If you sell two additional programs a month ($10,000) as a result

Self-publishing delivers the fastest ROI of time and money that you spend on your book. This is the absolute fundamental of the business-book strategy.

of your book, the investment will make you a $345,000 return over the three years. That is a 2200% ROI. End of debate.

Business book return on investment

Book investment	=	$19,000
Your speaker fee	=	$5,000
4 × speaker fee	=	$Break even
All speaker fees thereafter	=	$Profit

To choose, consider what you want to achieve

Go back to your Ultimate Guide to Getting Your Book Started. What do you want to achieve with your book? Choose wisely because traditional publishing takes your energy in a different direction to self-publishing.

Some may say self-publishing is vanity publishing (the pejorative term developed by publishers for people who chose to side-step their business). Publishers have convinced us all that self-published books cannot be as good as those selected by them. There is a risk that a self-published book might fall short. But times have changed. If you choose the right providers, the right editor, the right proofreader, the right designer and the right printer, there is no reason why you cannot achieve the standard of publishing today that you would achieve with a traditional publisher.

With guidance, self-publishing is easily done. However, there are quite a few decisions to be made. If you find it too challenging, you can go with a self-publishing service. These are fee-for-service providers who, for a package price, manage the editing, design and printing. There are many providers. Some include book distribution. For a fee, you remove stress from the production process.

Choosing an editor

Not all editors are the same, so choose your editor with care. There are many different types of editors. You're looking for a book editor who specialises in non-fiction books.

Don't be tempted to publish your book without working with an editor. Editors build your authority. Imagine your book comes back from the printer with spelling mistakes, typos, inconsistencies or structural errors. A good editor does more than eliminate such errors. They will address similar questions to those we asked your first readers, such as whether your message is clear and whether your target audience is clear.

They will also:

) Improve word quality, tone, awkward phrasing, flow and readability.

) Make your writing more engaging.

) Ensure consistent language and spelling.

) Make your style consistent.

) Make comments and suggestions about issues such as structural problems or weakness in expression.

Every so often I like to Google 'headline fails' for a laugh. I don't want you to be the person that we are laughing at.

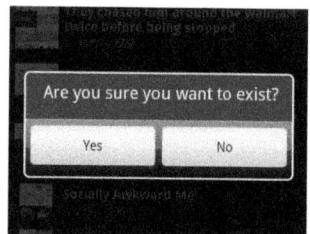

Back in 1987 in my misspent youth, I was a print-production manager in a graphic design studio, and part of my job was to get client work printed. Peter was the production manager at a printer we used. Every so often, clients wanted their job ridiculously fast. Rushing always leads to more mistakes. Our clients would approve a job for printing and when they received their 2000 copies back, discovered an error. Peter would say wistfully, 'Never enough time to print; always enough time to reprint.' So true.

When preparing your book, you might feel under enormous time and financial pressure. But if you print your book without this quality control and have to pull it, redesign it and reprint it as a result of errors, it can be financially devastating and undermine your authority. You may be tempted to ask your niece, nephew or someone in your family to do this job. Only do that if they are a qualified and experienced editor.

Here are 10 things to look for in your non-fiction book editor.

1. Comes recommended for non-fiction editing.

2. Has testimonials on their website.

3. Asks who the audience is for your book.

4. Gives a firm quote based on a review of your manuscript.

5. Uses a clear process and can guide you through it.

6. Starts with editing structure, then edits line by line.

7. Gives you constructive responses and suggests solutions.

8. Is a good communicator.

9. Listens to what you say.

10. Doesn't take over your book—they maintain your voice and your writing.

Proofreaders

Once the editing is done, I suggest you get a final proofread. Your editor may employ a proofreader. The proofreader is a last set of fresh eyes on your manuscript looking for mistakes. Have you ever noticed how errors creep into a document that you have read many times? It happens. All. The. Time.

How to choose a book designer

The design of your book is a determining factor in its success with your readers. The design is the vehicle for your words. Spend the time choosing the right vehicle to get your ideas to your readers. As with your editor, choose from designers experienced with book design. It can make a big difference to the price, and to the finished result.

Here are 10 things to look for in your non-fiction book designer.

1. Has done covers that you like.
2. Asks for examples of what you like.
3. Asks who the audience is for your book.
4. Can work with your preferred digital printer and understands epub options.
5. Can clearly explain the stages of the process.
6. Shows a portfolio of work on their website.
7. Listens to what you say.
8. Gives a firm quote based on a review of your manuscript and your brief.
9. Is clear on how many options and rounds of changes come with the quote.
10. Alerts you to extra fees for services such as illustrations or diagrams.

Start with the three principles of great book design

You must come to the designer with an idea of what you like, ideally examples. Consider these three principles to help narrow down your choice of design.

Principle 1: Books have genres and genres have conventions

Check out the colours and styles relevant to the business book genre by:

) googling other books on your topic

) checking a bookstore for other books on your topic.

Principle 2: Reader preference

Think about your reader and the books that might be on their shelf. What does your reader like?

Principle 3: Your preference

Now you have narrowed down the options, choose colours and styles from among these that you like. If you hate yellow, don't print your book in yellow even if your designer loves it. Choose colours, fonts and sizes that you like. To kick start your thoughts, consider your preferences in the following list:

) Simple

) Modern

) Luxury

) Playful

) Loud

) Feminine

) Pop

) Literal

) Detailed

) Retro

) Budget

) Serious

) Restrained

) Masculine

) Grunge

) Abstract

Questions your designer may ask you

) What size do you want your book to be?

) Do you need illustrations?

) What is your book title, and what else is going on your cover?

) Do you have illustrations, photos or diagrams, and are they print ready?

) Are you printing a hardback version?

) Is there anything you want to avoid? Colours, styles?

) What do you like? (Refer to the list on the previous page.)

The new printing options

Behind this whole process of self-publishing lies a revolution in printing technology: digital printing. This is the reason you have the power to step overnight into your authority by publishing a book.

Back when I was a print production manager in traditional offset printing, there was no such thing as print on demand. Print on demand means that you can print off a single copy of a book. In those days, it was impossible to justify the unit cost of a single book. A thousand copies would have been a small print run. Those in the vanguard of self-publishing before print on demand was available often discovered to their shock that one or two thousand books took up an entire second bedroom. Not an efficient use of space in your house, nor an efficient way of managing cashflow in your business.

With print on demand, there is only a marginal price premium for printing small quantities. It's extraordinary and exciting. I recommend no more than 200 books as a first run.

If you are planning to print 1000 or more copies of your book you might consider traditional (offset) printing. You must have a means of storing and distributing them quickly. If you've engaged a book distributor to get your books into bookshops it could be worth getting quotes from offset printers for that number of books.

Get a proof copy before you order

When you are ready to print, especially if you're managing it yourself, always print one copy to proof before ordering in a larger number. Even with all the checks and balances that you have—the first reader, the editor, the proofreader and the designer—errors happen. They will jump out at you when you get a printed copy. It's spooky, but it does happen. Always order one to proofread. Perhaps the trim of the book is too close to the writing. Perhaps the colour that you chose doesn't look right when you see it printed. Your designer can adjust it. Please, never ever order a print run without ordering a single copy to check first.

In a nutshell

Finishing is like magic dust that takes you from expert to authority. To finish, you need the help of an editor, a proofreader, a designer and a printer if you decide to self-publish. I've shown you how to get from go to whoa. There's nothing stopping you except your inner demon, and we've tackled how to get the demon on your side. Put aside your fear. Don't expect not to feel fear. Just put it aside and recognise that your book is an act of service, a gift to the world, and a huge accomplishment.

That's it. You are done. Now you've read this last chapter, nothing stands between you and the authority you deserve. Now it's over to you.

Over to you

Well, there you have it. Everything I know about writing a book, you know too. I didn't hold anything back. I want you to succeed and become a soldier in somebody's army, as international keynote speaker Vinh Giang would say (see his story in my introduction).

Could it be simpler? Start with who. Choose your best ideas. Organise them into a structure that makes them shine like diamonds. Flesh them out. Record your first draft. Polish your second draft using my seven steps. Then send your book to your first readers for feedback. Edit. Design. Print.

The difference between an expert and an authority is a book. In the dictionary, the words are interchangeable, but not in my world. (Author)ity is the mantle your book bestows on you. When you write your book, you step into a new zone. It's more public and more vulnerable. And, more powerful. As an author, your sphere of influence widens. More people will come to you, learn from you, and criticise you.

The move from expert to authority is one of changing identity. That is why it's so difficult. Once you publish your first book, you achieve that transformation. And with it comes a new demand. To write another one.

Your book is an awe-inspiring act of generosity to your readership, but it will bestow its gifts on you, too. You will gain more confidence and conviction in your expertise. Your ideas will shine with the clarity and quality that writing brings to them. One of the great joys of my work is watching authors step into the limelight. They win more clients with less work, they attract speaking gigs, they get busy. It's a big effort to be sure, but the rewards are enormous.

Writing a book is not for everyone. But for everyone who writes a book, my wish is that your book is the best it can be, and the first of many.

Stick to it.

Love, Kath

PS: *Got thoughts you'd like to share on this book? Email with the words* Overnight Authority *in the subject line (so you don't go to junk) and let me know. I'd love to hear from you. kath@kathwalters.com.au*

Publishing Success Case Studies

Leah Mather

Leah is the author of *Soft is the New Hard: How to Communicate Effectively Under Pressure.* As a speaker, trainer, coach and facilitator, she draws on her background in leadership, corporate communications and journalism to help executives, leaders and employees improve their communication, mindset and self-management.

> '*The book means I'm not just another comms person or leadership trainer in the market. I have intellectual property, a model and a structure that they can see works.*'

Leah's publishing journey

I wanted my book to be a supercharged business card that upped my credibility, so I could expand the clients I work with and up my prices for the programs and workshops I deliver. I also wanted a resource that participants in my training and workshops could take away and use to embed what they learned with me. Something they could use to keep reinforcing those lessons.

On top of that, though, I want to make a difference in people's lives. That's why I do what I do. And I knew that by upping my fees, I wasn't going to be as accessible to some of the people I used to work with. That didn't mean I was any less committed to helping people, and having a book meant helping anyone who needed it was still possible. Someone might not be able to afford to work with me, but they *can* buy the book, and then they have a practical resource in their hands.

Personally, I'm a voracious reader. What I think is special about a book is that the author's ideas and content are laid out in a structured way, in one place.

Sure, you can Google. Yes, you can find content in different places. But, when you're after more comprehensive learning, something that guides you on a journey, nothing beats a book.

My book has done very, very well. Not only is it selling, but I know people around the world are actually reading it, because they reach out to me. And I know that it's working to embed the lessons after workshops, because people tell me it is. The book takes the training from being a one-off to something that lasts.

I've had new clients call to say they've read the book, that they thought it was incredible and they want to work with me. But also, it works as a credibility piece—even with people who haven't read it. I was lucky in that it was a finalist in the Australian Career Book of the Year in 2020. That sort of acknowledgement just adds to the credibility.

Since the book came out, I've been able to focus what I offer, double my prices, and stay busy—even in the worst of COVID. The book means I'm not just another comms person or leadership trainer in the market. I have intellectual property, a model and a structure that they can see works.

Kath was brilliant with helping me to capture my unique voice. That voice says 'no bullshit,' and it works with the market I'm in. That market

It works as a credibility piece even with people who haven't read it.

Leah Mether

includes a lot of mining, power and water companies—industries that don't always have open arms to things like communications. Those guys often tell me that they haven't read a book for years or that they're not expecting mine to be any good. Then they read my book, and they like it, because there are heaps of stories and it's plain spoken. The book is practical and they connect with it. That makes the book a real selling tool for me if someone is wondering, 'Is she the right fit for this environment or not?'

As the author of this book, my positioning is rock solid. I'm working with organisations that maybe wouldn't have found me without the book, and my business has more than doubled. In a pandemic.

Peter Webb

Peter is an Australian organisational and integrative psychologist and leadership coach. He is the author of *System 3 Thinking: How to Choose Wisely When Facing Doubt, Dilemma, or Disruption*, based on his decades of research into how people choose wisely or foolishly.

'The voice I found through writing the book is one I didn't have before. That voice means my ideas have found a much wider audience than I ever thought possible. Today, I'm talking about these ideas to business and community leaders, as well as patients.'

Peter's publishing journey

My overnight success took about 15 years. That's about how long I had this book rattling around in my head. The idea came from seeing leaders and others make really awful decisions—decisions that affected employees, communities and sometimes the whole globe. I thought we could make the world a better place if we could just understand wisdom and how to apply it, so I started to research the psychology of wisdom.

I presented my findings in journals and at conferences and workshops. At the conferences and workshops, attendees would come up and ask, 'Where can we buy your book?' I eventually got sick of saying I hadn't written it yet.

There was another option, which was to take my research and turn it into a PhD, but I've seen people destroyed by the intensity of that process. Also, if you want to use your knowledge to consult or get speaking engagements, you have to turn your PhD thesis into some kind of book anyway. I thought, 'Why not cut out the middleman in that strategy and just write the book?'

That process of putting my research into a book turned out to be an amazing way to crystallise everything I've been talking about for years. It all came together in the book. It wasn't easy to start with. In fact, it was incredibly difficult to get out of the mode of writing for an academic audience. I needed to learn how to communicate my ideas to readers who want the essential elements. That audience wants to be entertained as well as informed. The readers of my book are different from the critical academic audience I was used to.

Through the process, Kath was firm with me that I had to write for a *single* reader. For me, it was a CEO I'd worked with for a few years, but holding onto that reader in my mind was hard through Melbourne's long lockdown. I kept saying to Kath, 'I've lost my reader, I don't know who I'm writing for.' She kept telling me, 'No, you're still writing for the same reader. Just keep writing.'

I came unglued there for a while, but eventually I found a voice that was appealing. Then writing became a joy, which it hasn't always been. Academic writing had been a slog.

The voice I found through writing the book is one I didn't have before. That voice means my ideas have found a much wider audience than I ever thought possible. Today, I'm talking about these ideas to business and community leaders, as well as patients.

In my mind, the book was going to be a sophisticated business card. It's proved to be much more than that. The feedback has been a bit overwhelming, to be honest. But it means I know the book has a home. People who need to read it are reading it, and they're getting a lot out of it.

At the same time, I'm being paid to run workshops—invitations that are a direct result of the book. It's not too much to say that having the book has opened an entirely new vista for me—one I didn't even know existed. One thing I've learned is that writing a book does something intangible to your concept of yourself—how you see yourself and perceive yourself in the world. It's not a linear thing. It's not, 'Oh, I've written a book.' It's the process, all the slicing and dicing. Then coming out the other end and realising you've got an audience that you didn't have before.

That self-development journey has turned out to be far more valuable to me than trying to get a return on my investment from selling books. I've changed myself, my ideas, my perception of myself, and my ideas about what I'm capable of.

And then there's a glorious moment when you open your first box of books,[1] and you're picking up *your* book for the first time, holding it and smelling the pages. That was absolutely extraordinary.

Genevieve Hawkins

Genevieve is a senior executive at one of Australia's best-known companies. She is the author of *Mentally at Work*, a book for leaders who want to get ahead of the curve in connecting performance, leadership and the mental health of themselves and their teams.

> *'Before the book, I could see a risk of being painted into a corner from a work perspective. The book got me out of that. When I'm ready, I have the credibility to be on a speaking circuit, seeing the world.'*

---

1 Peter has a nice picture on his homepage of this moment: www.peterjwebb.com.

And then there's a glorious moment when you open your first box of books, and you're picking up your book for the first time, holding it and smelling the pages. That was absolutely extraordinary.

Peter Webb

Genevieve's publishing journey

Well before COVID hit, I could see the tsunami coming. It was clear that the developed world was going to have all sorts of problems with mental illness. That was scary and I was frustrated with the way people were thinking about the problem. My own team were saying to me, 'You need to pull this stuff out from your brain and put it on paper. That way, you can scale the advice you can give and the impact you can have on people.'

That's why I wrote the book, to help senior leaders connect the dots between science, systems thinking and leadership. A book that they could keep referring back to with sticky notes throughout.

I would have been happy if a few leaders had said to me the book had changed the way they chose to lead. That would have been a pretty awesome thing. Beyond that, I hoped to recoup my investment. But both things happened faster than I would have imagined.

Since publishing the book, I've been brought in by a range of organisations, including McKinsey, to work with leadership teams. We go through the issues I talk about in the book, and we work out what practical steps they can take. These engagements can mean selling up to 400 copies of the book per session, as well as the fee for speaking. Pretty quickly, every single book I sell and every single speaking gig has been extra because the costs were covered. At this stage, I'm not looking to be a speaker full time. I've got a role that's perfect—crazy and awesome. I do this speaking and coaching as an additional piece of my career. Having said that, before the book I could see a risk of being painted into a corner from a work perspective. The book got me out of that. There is just a whole other level of credibility that comes with being an author of a book, versus writing articles and doing podcasts. I feel a strong sense of purpose about contributing to reversing the trend on mental illness in the developed world. The book has given me the confidence to continue to make career

There's just a whole other level of credibility that comes with being an author of a book.

Genevieve Hawkins

decisions around that sense of purpose, and it's opened up more options of where my career might go.

It's not really about selling piles of books. Very few people sell piles of books. A book is about positioning yourself as a thought leader. And for me that was about helping leaders, reinventing myself, and giving myself freedom for whatever the next thing is.

The process of writing the book was much easier than I expected because Kath got me crystal clear on my audience. That was one reason I'd struggled with writing before—I was writing for too many audiences.

If you'd asked me before the book what my wildest dream with this book would be, I'd have told you it would be Brené Brown interviewing me. Today, I have a US publicist telling me there's a 50/50 chance of that happening, and I am so excited about the prospect. But more importantly, I am humbled by the feedback I'm getting from people I know and don't know about how this book has helped them be mentally healthy and a better leader. That's a legacy I am proud of.

Mike Adams

Mike is the author of *Seven Stories Every Salesperson Must Tell*. An engineer by training, Mike became a sales leader in multiple industries he knew nothing about at the start. He found the only way to succeed was to find the right business stories to tell to the right people at the right time. Today, he trains sales teams around the world in the methods laid out in his book.

Mike's publishing journey

'From the book, they can see I'm credible. The result is that I'm working with a lot more multinationals and my fees have tripled.'

I'm an engineer who became a successful salesperson by using the right story at the right time. That's what my book is about. I'll tell you I wrote the book so that my consulting and training business had collateral to give to CEOs and sales leaders. However, I suspect the real reason is probably something to do with satisfying my ego—looking good to my friends and stuff like that.

I'll admit to some dreams about my book being a bestseller, but I knew that was pretty unlikely. Mostly, I wrote the book for myself. By writing our ideas down, we're explaining things to ourselves, which is quite fundamental to developing ideas.

The book actually did pretty well. I get messages from people all over the world, and it's up to about 130 reviews on Amazon, which is definitely better than average. Plus, every now and then I'll get a pretty big cheque when someone's obviously ordered 50 or 100 of the books for their sales team.

That's still happening, although the book was published in 2018.

You can't have coffees with people overseas until they get comfortable with the idea of working with you. With the book, I'm able to reach out to companies overseas and the book gets them comfortable. From the book, they can see I'm credible. The result is that I'm working with a lot more multinationals and my fees have tripled. I also know there are people selling consulting and sales training based on my book. I'm good with that because an idea is more important than the person that created it. The people who use my book to sell consulting and training are promoting the idea of storytelling as a technique. They're offering a method for salespeople to be not quite so shit at their job. That was my objective. And anyway, I like to think there's no way you can read my book and do sales training the way I do it.

Even though I collect, write and tell stories for a living, the book might not have been written without Kath's framework. I probably had an overinflated idea of my ability to write a book, and I'm the kind of person who likes to put things off. Working with a coach was something of a commitment strategy. If I didn't have someone keeping me accountable, it was probably never going to happen. And I did like the idea that the 90-day framework meant it would be done quickly.

Now that I have written the book, it's like a fabulous thing has happened to me: I've written a book that other sales trainers admire. That has made me fantastic connections all around the world with people I never thought I'd be having conversations with. One of them was Michael Bosworth, who wrote *Solution Selling*, which is a classic. After I finished *Seven Stories*, I found his address and sent him the manuscript. He actually read it and liked it so much that agreed to write the foreword. Then he narrated it in the audiobook version. If you'd told me that writing a book would lead to things like that, I wouldn't have believed you.

Mary Freer

Mary helps leaders create high-quality, compassionate, creative, innovative and productive workplaces. She is a Westpac Bicentennial Social Change Fellow, a Member of the Australian Compassion Council, a TEDx speaker, a coach at Seth Godin's AltMBA and the author of *Compassion Revolution: Start Now. Use what You Have. Keep Going.*

Mary's publishing journey

'What's taken me by surprise is the assumptions people make about me, my expertise and what I have to offer because I have written a book.'

I wrote a book for a few reasons. Firstly, I wanted to reach a much wider audience. Also, people often wanted to engage with me just to hear about the basics of how compassion and compassionate leadership could make a difference in the health ecosystem. So, rather than me having to go through that same kind of explanation every time, I wrote the book.

If you'd told me that writing a
book would lead to things like that,
I wouldn't have believed you.

Mike Adams

The other reason was that people in middle-management positions in hospitals and large healthcare services would ring me to say they wanted to put the idea forward to work with me. They wanted me to help them to do that by giving them the science or a great story to tell. And I used to do all that. Then I thought, 'You know what, it'd be a whole lot easier if I wrote a book'. Once I had the book, I could just say, 'I'll send you the book!' or 'Have you bought the book?'

What happened once I'd written the book was that people would not only grab the book for themselves, but also they would buy it for their executives. They were using the book in the way that I used it with them, so the book turned out to be a great solution.

I already had a podcast, but in a podcast, I can only engage people in short bursts. I couldn't look into their organisation and know what it was that they needed to mount their argument or to put forward their proposal. The difference with the book is that I've collected everything and put it together in one place. Now, they can go to the book and find the bit they need.

Since writing the book, I've come to understand the world is strangely divided into people who've written a book, and people who haven't. And what's really taken me by surprise is the assumptions people who haven't written a book make about me, my expertise and what I have to offer because I have written a book. People didn't introduce me as 'Mary records a podcast,' but they do introduce me as 'Mary's written a book.' There's just something about the actual writing of a book that brings credibility.

Secretly, I probably thought that about people who'd written a book as well. So there's something that being an author has done to the level of confidence with which I approach my work—'Just listen to me for a minute because I wrote a book.'

The book was my first experience of writing in long form. I've written a blog and I've worked as an academic, but that's a different sort of

The *British Medical Journal* is calling me because they read the book and want me to be their plenary speaker.

Mary Freer

writing. This was a different process, and it felt really new to me. I had to find a way to do it in a rhythm. That was not something that I knew about, and I had a go at writing it on my own, but it turned out I needed Kath's structured way of doing it. On my own, I was creating a lot of short essays that I thought would form a book, but in reality the essay part never ended. I could have spent the rest of my life writing those essays and never got to a book.

The truth is that I don't like being kind of disciplined or coached by someone else. But I do love being a coach. There are lots of times where I was like, 'Don't tell me what to do.' But I stuck with it because the promise was, if you stick with it, you will have a book. So I stuck with it and finished on time. It takes discipline.

The result is that people in different places in the world are reading the book and I now get more invitations to speak. Next week, I'm the keynote at the British Medical Journal International Forum. In my world, healthcare, that's a pretty significant conference. Speaking at the forum is particularly meaningful to me because six years ago I won a fellowship. The highlight of that fellowship was travelling to the BMJ conference to listen to the speakers. Fast forward six years, and the BMJ is calling *me* because they read the book and want me to be their plenary speaker.

Since writing the book, I've employed someone to work with me, so things are happening that I wouldn't have been in a position to do a few years ago.

If you've got a book that you want to write and you can discipline yourself and find the rhythm, you can definitely write it.

Books Mentioned in this Book

Here's a list of all the books I mentioned in case you want to explore any of them.

Ace Your Medical Exams Patsy Tremayne

Angela's Ashes Frank McCourt

Big Magic: Creative Living Beyond Fear Elizabeth Gilbert

Book Blueprint Jacqui Pretty

Build Live Give Paul Higgins

Compassion Revolution: Start now. Use what you have. Keep going
    Mary Freer

Courageous Sponsorship Annie Sheehan

Epic Content Marketing Joe Pulizzi

Everybody Writes Ann Handley

Fully Cooked Samuel Eddy

How to Win Friends and Influence People Dale Carnegie

How to Write Short Roy Peter Craft

I never metaphor I didn't like Dr Mardy Grothe

Logical Leadership Jenny Bailey

Made to Stick Chip and Dan Heath

Man's Search for Meaning Viktor Frankl

Mentally at Work Genevieve Hawkins

Purple Cow Seth Godin

Smart Work Dermot Crowley

Soft is the New Hard Leah Mether

Speakership: The art of oration, the science of influence Matt Church

Sticky Content: The delicate art of content marketing Kath Walters

Start with Why Simon Sinek

Stop Doubting, Start Leading Leonie Green

Story Mastery: How leaders supercharge results with business storytelling Yamini Naidu

System 3 Thinking: How to choose wisely when facing doubt, dilemma, or disruption Peter Webb

The 4-Hour Workweek Tim Ferris

The Adversity Advantage Claudia Lantos

The Elements of Style W Strunk and EB White

The Four-Day Work Week Andrew Barnes

The How of Habits Bri Williams

The Liberated Organisation Joan Lurie

The Purpose Project Carolyn Tate

The Seven Habits of Highly Effective People Stephen Covey

The Seven Stories Every Salesperson Must Tell Mike Adams

The Shredder Test: A step-by-step guide to writing WINNING proposals Robyn Haydon

The Subtle Art of Not Giving a F*ck Mark Manson

The Tipping Point Malcolm Gladwell

The True Believers Christina Guidotti

This Book Means Business Alison Jones

Value: How to talk about what you do so people want to buy it Robyn Haydon

Weasel Words Don Watson

Write like Hemingway Dr Andrew Wilson

www.ingramcontent.com/pod-product-compliance
Lightning Source LLC
Chambersburg PA
CBHW040754220326
41597CB00029BA/4809